SONATA
MULATTICA

SONATA MULATTICA

A Life in Five Movements and a Short Play

poems by

RITA DOVE

W. W. NORTON & COMPANY

New York • London

For information about permission to reproduce selections from this book,
write to Permissions, W. W. Norton & Company, Inc.,
500 Fifth Avenue, New York, NY 10110

For information about special discounts for bulk purchases, please contact
W. W. Norton Special Sales at specialsales@wwnorton.com or 800-233-4830

Manufacturing by The Haddon Craftsmen, Inc.
Book design by Chris Welch
Production manager: Anna Oler

Library of Congress Cataloging-in-Publication Data

Dove, Rita.
Sonata mulattica : a life in five movements and a short play /
poems by Rita Dove.—1st ed.
p. cm.
Includes bibliographical references.
ISBN 978-0-393-07008-8
I. Title.
PS3554.O884S66 2009
811'.54—dc22

2008054281

ISBN 978-0-393-33893-5 pbk.

W. W. Norton & Company, Inc.
500 Fifth Avenue, New York, N.Y. 10110
www.wwnorton.com

W. W. Norton & Company Ltd.
Castle House, 75/76 Wells Street, London W1T 3QT

3 4 5 6 7 8 9 0

For Fred & Aviva . . . always

Contents

III

STURM UND DRANG

VOLKSTHEATER:
A SHORT PLAY FOR THE COMMON MAN

IV

"ALL IS ASHES"

V
NOMADIA

EPILOGUES

Preface

Two centuries ago the violinist George Augustus Polgreen Bridgetower, son of a white mother and a self-styled "African prince," rose to his fifteen minutes of fame. He might have become one of the most revered musical virtuosos of all time . . . had he not crossed swords with his mercurial mentor, Ludwig van Beethoven. What's known today as the Kreutzer Sonata was originally dedicated to Beethoven's new "mulatto" friend, who premiered it in Vienna to wide acclaim, the ink barely dry on the composer's pages. So far, so good; but oh, if only George—all but twenty-three years of age—had shown better judgment and not blatantly ogled the object of Ludwig's affections!

This great cautionary anecdote is true. My tale is woven from historical events just as surely as the incidental details have been subjected to literary imagination. All the principal players once lived real lives—Mad King George and his spendthrift son "Prinny," court lady Charlotte Papendiek and Miklós the Magnificent, "Papa" Haydn and Emperor Napoleon, concert impresario Johann Salomon and street fiddler Black Billy Waters. Even Thomas Jefferson makes a cameo appearance, attending (as the record shows) a Bridgetower concert in Paris mere months before the French Revolution erupts. Little George was nine at the time; as for Sally Hemings being in the audience . . . well, here I claim poetic license.

—*Rita Dove*
Charlottesville, Virginia
Fourth of July, 2008

PROLOGUES

"Begin at the beginning," the King said very gravely,
"and go on till you come to the end: then stop."
—*Alice's Adventures in Wonderland*

The Bridgetower

per il Mulatto Brischdauer
gran pazzo e compositore mulattico
—Ludwig van Beethoven, 1803

If was at the Beginning. If
he had been older, if he hadn't been
dark, brown eyes ablaze
in that remarkable face;
if he had not been so gifted, so young
a genius with no time to grow up;
if he hadn't grown up, undistinguished,
to an obscure old age.
If the piece had actually been,
as Kreutzer exclaimed, unplayable—even after
our man had played it, and for years
no one else was able to follow—
so that the composer's fury would have raged
for naught, and wagging tongues
could keep alive the original dedication
from the title page he shredded.

Oh, if only Ludwig had been better-looking,
or cleaner, or a real aristocrat,
von instead of the unexceptional van
from some Dutch farmer; if his ears
had not already begun to squeal and whistle;
if he hadn't drunk his wine from lead cups,
if he could have found True Love. Then
the story would have held: In 1803
George Polgreen Bridgetower,
son of Friedrich Augustus the African Prince
and Maria Anna Sovinki of Biala in Poland,
traveled from London to Vienna
where he met the Great Master

who would stop work on his Third Symphony
to write a sonata for his new friend
to premiere triumphantly on May 24,
whereupon the composer himself
leapt up from the piano to embrace
his "lunatic mulatto."

Who knows what would have followed?
They might have palled around some,
just a couple of wild and crazy guys
strutting the town like rock stars,
hitting the bars for a few beers, a few laughs . . .
instead of falling out over a girl
nobody remembers, nobody knows.

Then this bright-skinned papa's boy
could have sailed his fifteen-minute fame
straight into the record books—where
instead of a Regina Carter or Aaron Dworkin or Boyd Tinsley
sprinkled here and there, we would find
rafts of black kids scratching out scales
on their matchbox violins so that some day
they might play the impossible:
Beethoven's Sonata No. 9 in A Major, Op. 47,
also known as The Bridgetower.

Prologue of the Rambling Sort

This is a tale of light and shadow,
what we hear and the silence that follows.
Remember this as we set out
across sea and high roads, as talk turns
to gentlemen and valets, grave robbers
and tormented souls. This is a story
about music and what it does to those
who make it, whom it enslaves . . . yes,
slavery of all kinds enters into the mix,
although the skin of our protagonist
does not play so great a role
in his advancement and subsequent
fade from grace as might be imagined.
Or does it? Rather, let us say that
the racial divide has not yet been invented;
you lived, you died, things happened
between the two.
                           But you are here
for the story. The story someone penned
in thirst and anger on an uncharted desert isle,
then stuffed into a bottle that now floats,
a glassine porpoise, swell upon swell, too small
for anyone to find . . . until the paper inside
finally crisps, tanned beyond recognition
by the sun that is its constant lover. . . .
So it is a lost story
but we will be imagining it, anyway.
We'll leave out the boring parts.
There'll be marching bands, wardrobe changes
and, of course, Love—melting hearts,

sweaty meringues, Flowers of the Realm
and the occasional heave-to in the shrubbery.
Political cartoons. Honorable,
quiet fools.
                    The major players:
father and son, son and father.
Two composers, a violinist between them.
An African Prince in Turkish robes;
a Prince of Wales turned Regent turned King;
an Assistant Keeper of the Wardrobe to the Queen.
(Always the wait-staff, ever vigilant, eye- and ear-y.)
A music student turned copyist, a performer
turned entrepreneur, a faux emperor, a famed chef,
a fiddling beggar; plus assorted fops and dabblers,
countesses and dwarves, all with their freakish
bundles of *accoutrements*: turbans and reticules,
wigs and vinaigrettes; brooches painted
in the shape of the lover's eye.
                              Enter
two prodigies (of an age but not a color),
an absent mother and all-too-present father,
a fattening son and his maddening sire,
a small man and his indigestion,
a fat man and his gout,
rabble and revolutionaries,
guillotines cranking up in time
with the organ-grinders—just
your average gulp of hope
and gobble of terror—then picture a river
pouring itself through a city,

picking up garbage and gulls,
doused in barge oil, speckled with swans,
lapping and sloshing and pooling . . .
that's how we'll be traveling—and the rest,
as they say, is background music.
(Ah, but what heavenly music *that* was. . . .)

I

THE PRODIGY

Un début curieux, & qui a infiniment intéresse, c'est celui de M. Bridge-Tower, jeune Nègre des Colonies, qui a joué plusieurs concertos de violon avec une netteté, une facilité, une exécution & même une sensibilité, qu'il est bien rare de rencontrer dans un age si tendre (il n'a pas dix ans). Son talent, aussi vrai que précose, est une des meilleures réponses que l'on puisse faire aux Philosophes qui veulent priver ceux de sa Nation & de sa couleur, de la faculté de se distinguer dans les Arts.

[A curious debut, & one of infinite interest, is that of Mr. Bridge-Tower, young Negro from the Colonies, who has performed several violin concertos with a clarity, facility, execution & sensitivity that is quite rare to encounter at so tender an age (he is not yet ten years old). His talent, as genuine as it is precocious, is one of the best responses one can make to those Philosophers that seek to deprive those of his Nation & color of the opportunity to distinguish themselves in the Arts.]

—*Le Mercure de France*, 1789

(Re)Naissance

*February 29, 1780. Peasants in the field, digging for
the last of the frostbitten potato crop. No angel appears.*

Snow's a gentle pillager: It sucks
where we have no more rags to bind,
seeks out our furthest tips to freeze
in reprimand. From the East
an icy flourish reminds us
how meager an essence we harbor:
mere blood and burbling humors
trussed into a package of skin.

Each booted stride
a cracking:
            trudge, slip, o woeful
            processional. This is

our lot. Our staged creation:
whiteness billowing, fuzzed silence sliced
by a woman—one scream
only, quickly held back.
She is one of us, a peasant
mindful of the body's purpose:
Be strong, survive.

Bundled in the season's last rags,
all tufts and breath-sodden fringes,
we permit a brief yearning
to burn deep in the gut
on this day of no accounting,
no different than yesterday or tomorrow,
and then the answering cry, all but muted
by the western wind . . . tiny, enraged.

That's it, then. Another soul
quickened to misery,
dark as our shadows lurching
over the snow-riddled furrows.
Another spirit cursed to walk
this glacial crust, another body
some day to bury.

Capriccio

Miklós the Magnificent,
otherwise known as Nikolaus Josef
of the clan Salamon in the Czallóköz
and successor to the seat of Esterházy in Galanta,
royal instigator of the Baroque castle at Fertöd,
Lieutenant Field Marshall of the Austrian Empire (decorated),
musician (practiced), sober, honest,
and educated by Jesuits,

had a fantasy: to assemble
an array of Nature's eccentricities—
a dwarf, an African, perhaps a gypsy
or ferocious Turk or flat-faced Borneo,
summoning each before him
dressed in the deep blue and red livery
of the House of Esterházy
to see who among them would bear
with the most decorum
the imperial trappings.

He would hold a masquerade.
Haydn could work up an opera.

All this transpired within a crescent of ochre stone
run aground in the marshlands
of Neusiedlersee, rural
western Hungary,
in the year
1785.

Friedrich Augustus Bridgetower Discovers the Purposes of Fatherhood

The boy is smitten with tiny sounds:
purring bees and crickets, sighing leaves,
hammer clack from the courtyard.
(Will those flagstones ever finish?)
Last evening I managed to shoo him off

seconds before the Prince
exited the belvedere on his way
in to dine: This time
the royal tapered heels tip-tapping
had mesmerized. I apologized

with my most flamboyant bow
(guaranteed to coax a smile).
Now Pater Niemecz has volunteered
to attend this strange rapture;
all morning from the library

an infernal peeping—
mechanical clocks blasting the ether
with their toy fife parade!
No nervous solicitudes can muffle
this noise nor genuflection deliver

a reprieve—here's Maestro Haydn,
fresh from his daily audience,
striding across the marble
in full *Kapellmeister* livery
to investigate our misery's

source: Tomorrow . . . tomorrow,
gods willing, if there is a tomorrow . . .
I'll arrange to send the boy north,
back to Saxony, so his mother
can do the sorting. First, though,

there's the small matter
of this approaching tribunal,
Pater, *Meister*, and Youngblood—
my *petit terror* smiling
up at me, caught in the thrall

of his bright brown
ignorance. Master Haydn
reaches down to cup
the rough head, murmurs:
There's music in here.

Ach, is that so?
Then, by your Lordship's
grace and the sacred
lyre of Apollo,
let's squeeze it out of him!

Lines Whispered to a Pillow

Staff Quarters, Esterházy Estate

Little monkey, little cow,
Can you hear me listening? Now:
Ticking clock, piano plink—
Watch me hear you, feel me think.

Recollection, Preempted

I remember crickets, hidden,
       singing from the green
             globes of shrubbery.
Combed gravel, curved kilometers
         of ash-gray rivulets
                  not-to-be-played-on.

         Woodland fairies beckoning

                         away

away

        from the eternal drone
           of the baryton—

        meaning Papa Haydn
        was out composing in the shed
        by the horse stables: dread work,

    all for the musical Prince.

        (I was told some of these things.)

Heat. An entire afternoon
    spent in choking dust,
        teams of servants lighting jars of black tallow
           along the palace steps, all to make
    a starry bridge
         at nightfall
         when the guests arrived

for one of Papa's amusements—
ceaseless operas, human and marionette:
inconsequential music, even to a boy's ears.

               (The puppet theater
          was my favorite hiding place:
               dark but glimmering,
                    a cave inside
                    a treasure chest.
               I sang to myself.
          It was like being buried
                    in jewels.)

But oh, the witchery of orchestral strings—
          the full *body* of sound gathering you in,
                    as to a mother's bosom
                    or a haystack at sunset,
                         to plunge into
               that stinging embrace . . .

                              (I was caught listening
                         and given a toy violin.)

That last year in heaven,
          the withering prince
crammed every crevice of time
with farces—as if to laugh
          were health itself:

Barbiere di Siviglia,
Paisiello's *L'amor contrastato;*
Cimarosa's *Il credulo* and
L'impresario in angustie.

I remember this, I do!
When we were told to leave
I committed the season's program to memory.
"Glory for us, boy," Father growled;
"away from this hinterland!"
   But I saw the triumph
   in the head porter's frown,
   and dwarf Johann weeping
   along the road, tiny
   under his bulging pack.

       Papa Haydn in a waistcoat,
        standing by the shed.

I confess, I don't know why I lie so.
   We were far away
by then—beyond Paris and the revolution,
   beyond even my sensational debuts
    at Brighton and Bath.

Paris, Panting

A curious debut, & one of infinite interest, is that of Mr. Bridge-Tower,
young Negro from the Colonies . . .

—Le Mercure de France, *1789*

At nine years, the youth astonishes
for his maturity of playing.
We at Le Mercure *celebrate his arrival*
to the Parisian concert stage.

They say leap-year babies
are out-of-time, moony. I'm really
just two birthdays' old, closer to the womb
than this world.

He was presented by his father, the Moor
Friedrich Augustus, to whom much praise is due.

Praise me. I am small. This hall looms
nearly as large and dark as he.

What Doesn't Happen

The notion that the carriage wheels clattering through Paris
remind him of the drums from the islands in his father's tales:
clickclack sputterwhir—he could make a song of it, dance
this four-in-hand down the cobbles of the rue du Bac
as he balances his small weight against the pricking cushions
clacksputter whir—all the cadences jumbled together
except the thudding dirge of his heart.

That he can see, in curtained twilight, the violin case in his lap
twitch with every jounce, like an animal trapped under the hunter's eye;
that he can sense, down shrouded alleys, danger rustling just as surely
as he can feel spring's careless fingers feathering his chest and smell
April's ferment in the stink of the poor marching toward him. . . .

Though none of this is true. He hears nothing but clatter.
He can't see the rain-slicked arc of the bridge passing under him
as the pale stone of the palace rears up and he climbs down
to be whisked into the massive *Salle des Machines*,
his father's cloak folded back like a bat's tucked wing—

because it was a dry spring that year on the Continent.

Nonetheless, he ignores his heart's thudding and steps out
onto the flickering stage, deep and treacherous
as a lake still frozen at sunset, aglow with reflected light.
Soon the music will take him across; he'll feel each string's ecstasy
thrum in his head and only then dare to open his eyes to gaze
past the footlights at the rows of powdered curls
(*let's see the toy bear jump his hoops!*)
nodding, lorgnettes poised, not hearing but judging—

except for that tall man on the aisle, with hair
the orange of fading leaves; and the two girls beside him—
one a younger composition of snow and embers,
but the other—oh the other dark, dark yet warm
as the violin's nut-brown sheen . . . miraculous creature
who fastens her solemn black gaze on the boy as if to say
you are what I am, what I yearn to be—

so that he plays only for her and not her keepers;
and when he is finally free to stare back,
applause rippling over the ramparts—even then
she does not smile.

Windsor

I was told to practice
out of sight, in the servants' wing.
I was also required to execute
a gentleman's curtsy, deep as a girl's—
stick the left leg out and sweep my arm
as if whisking an imaginary hat
from an imaginary powdered wig.

I've always wanted such a hat,
with three corners and crests
and a towering plume. *Someday,*
Father says, meaning *Be still.*
But I am! So quiet, from the shadows
I can hear a maid's shushed giggle;
I can listen to the concertmaster's
muttered grunts and wheezes
without once blurting: *Papa Haydn
wouldn't rush so, he says each note
deserves its appointed terrain. . . .*

I am to appear at the Queen's Lodge
promptly at seven, make my gentleman's bow
and play the Viotti Concerto.
So many glittering halls! And secret passageways
strung behind them to travel through
like favored mice between the walls.
Windsor: Every phrase ends with it,
each whisper another wondrous layer—
*You're quite the lucky lad to be here;
the feather in your cap, boy, remember*

Windsor—and on and on, until the word
grows its own breeze, Father's robes swirling
as I follow—*hurry, boy!*—over Middle Ward
and out the iron castle gate: I can see
the Lodge now, a dim brown snag
plopped square and dark across the longest path
anyone could ever imagine.

Struck dumb? Always happens
the first time.

It makes me think of ships,
of travel: a line slicing the soft green,
God's whip lash straight down
the heaving back of England . . .

The Long Walk at Windsor:
all the world at His Majesty's feet!

No. Mine, in these pinch-buttoned shoes.
All the world left behind,
not the world I am walking toward
now.

Mrs. Papendiek's Diary (1)

Preparations for the winter included procuring
thick stuff for warm petticoats, plus
the sewing of four great coats, dark blue,
with matching rows of small gold buttons
for the children—who looked,
in the words of Mrs. Burke, "winning."
The Queen remarked upon them as well,
commending me for managing always
to outfit them in a manner both elegant
and unassuming. I was overcome by her kindness.

We were invited to Her Majesty's Lodge
to hear the newest musical prodigy.
Young violinist Bridgetower arrived at Windsor
accompanied by his father, an African
yet a man of discernment and varied tastes,
exquisite deportment and considerable
beauty of form. The son, a lad of ten or twelve,
bore a hue that seemed cast in darkest bronze;
he was smartly dressed, possessed an admirable
restraint, and played the Viotti Concerto
with an eloquence and refinement
rarely delivered by his more celebrated seniors.

Afterwards we enjoyed a light supper
of cold meats and poultry, followed by sweets.
The father Bridgetower entertained the table
with his judicious and amusing observations;
he knows several languages and seems at home
in the world. I was glad to be wearing

the yellow Indian muslin over white petticoats,
with purple straps and gold embroidery
along the veil, arranged *en toque*,
which drew compliments from all present,
including the Moor.

The Marine Pavilion, Brighthelmston

Take a square box, the sides of which are three feet and a half, and the height
a foot and a half. Take a large Norfolk turnip, cut off the green of the leaves, . . .
and put the turnip on the middle of the top of the box. Then take four turnips
of half the size, treat them in the same way, and put them on the corners of the
box. Then take a considerable number of the bulbs of the crown imperial, the
narcissus, the hyacinth, the tulip, the crocus, and others; let the leaves of each
have sprouted to about an inch, more or less according to the size of the bulb; put
all these, pretty promiscuously, but pretty thickly, on the top of the box. Then
stand off and look at your architecture. There! . . . as to what you ought to put
in the box, that is a subject far above my cut.

—*William Cobbett*, Rural Rides *(1822)*

More than a dream, more than longing,
the banner of scent fading
as you advance, fifty years
to completion but always ahead
by half a whiff, one blink of
a weary eye, one tear's sting
as the field brightens, blurs . . . oh if only.
More than all that.
More than brocade's parabolic flashes and shadows.
More than a lorgnette dangling from the perfect manicure,
saffron's burning filaments shaken
from a diminutive tube,
wisps and whiskers,
dream within a dream, perhaps not even that . . .
you need to imagine yourself larger
than the country you occupy. You need to make
others understand what you have glimpsed,
against the morning sky, inside a nutshell,
its singular beauty—the perforated towers
like granite lace, the roof a garden of domes and spires,
voluptuous, riotous . . . too extravagant
for this fishing village, indeed too extravagant
for Britain, but this is how lavish a spirit
a great nation must offer! Clouds, after all, are more

than bearers of rain. The infinite sea
moves inside us; each morsel placed on the tongue awakens
the perfumes and sediments of its origins.
There can never be enough pleasure.
To deny ourselves the prospect of ravishment
is to be cursed to gnash our pitiable path
through existence, to squeal when fed and bray
when kicked. People, feast upon this
miracle—such beauty shining
almost weightless above
the net-strewn encampments of the whelk eaters;
this vision a promise from your King-to-be:
proof that each of us bears inside
a ruinous, monumental love.

The Wardrobe Lesson

Everyone in this brine-soused village
believes an African loves color—so let it be
red for our promenade along the Steyne,
with a splash of yellow
to inflame their watery sensibilities.
I think it's the sun they so yearn for;
blue saddens this close to the sea, though
turquoise is beckoning and emerald's best
a hue entertained only in furnishings. True,

we are props of a sort, let's not forget it;
yet what an aspect we'll project
unleashed among the masses!
Against our darker palette, any color thrills.
The main thing is fabric and plenty of it:
clouds of silk, waves of damask
to be cast off or furled neat to the chest
with a certain, sly emphasis. . . .

You'll learn these sophistications in time.
For now, it's enough to remember
we are here to confound them,
these wizened polyps crossing the sands
in their creaking bathing machines!
So: bright sashes and billowing sleeves,
rings on as many fingers as you dare,
perhaps a turban or some other headdress
to lend majesty without competing.

The ladies *adore* a cape. Different
from a cloak, this you can wear inside,
where one brisk swirl will conjure a fable
of perfumed trysts and moonlit swordplay.
As for the embroidered slippers—ungainly
as they might seem, the upturned toes
do not emasculate. Each step becomes
necessarily deliberate, and so recalls

the boudoir.
                    Don't flinch! It won't do
to ignore what waits behind each smile—
that unvoiced sigh, accompanying
your every tremolo! Go ahead, examine
those upturned faces in the concert hall,
their tiny gasps and glistening cheeks. . . .
I've seen it, boy, even for one young as you.

Ah, the ladies are always bored and lonely.

You will not need a horse if you have a cape.

Mrs. Papendiek's Diary (2)

Embittered negotiations with the King's musicians have led
to the regrettable situation in which I found myself
this morning. To begin, the benefit concert intended to announce
young Bridgetower to musical society
could not find adequate orchestral accompaniment;
the petition was rejected summarily by the royal musicians,
who steadfastly refuse to play extra musical events
ever since the King had dismissed their appeal
to be allowed employment off royal payroll;
this standoff was resolved by Mr. Papendiek's offer
to host the concert at our house: and so to me
fell the task of supervising ticket sales, refreshment,
the arrangement of furniture, and the like.

But Time will neither race nor tarry, and so all was sorted out.
The guests arrived in high spirits—and with some surprises;
protocol was smoothed over as best as circumstances permitted.
Mrs. Jervois shone in her purple silk and gold-worked cape;
I had settled on my muslin dress with jacket,
graced by a chip hat trimmed in deep mazarin blue,
as befitting the hostess for the evening.
The entertainments began—a flute quartet
followed by a glee, and then the Viotti Concerto
played by young Bridgetower, who sparkled with pathos.
I could tell others were as deeply affected
at the prospect of such talent among us.

As the children could not be admitted officially
(for that would take seats away from paying subscribers),
my little Fred curled up on the floor, his back against the sofa,

for the first Act; and when the maid came looking
slid under and stayed there, through refreshments
and Clementi's Duet in C, which opened the second Act;
after which he rose to kiss me and went sweetly off to bed.
There followed more singing, two quartets with Bridgetower,
a symphony, and it was over—except for refreshments
up and down stairs, and a late supper for the performers.
Although I retired when the ladies departed,
I could hear the men laughing well into the night.

The Seaside Concerts

Bath Morning Post, *December 8, 1789*

Saturday morning last the citizens of Bath hailed the debut
of a phenomenal musical talent: the mulatto George Bridgetower,
in concert at the New Assembly Rooms. Aged only ten, the youth
astonished all with his maturity of rendition and technical perfection;
our own Rauzzini, whose mindful generosity toward public entertainment
should be extolled at every opportunity, declared he had never heard
such execution before. Those fortunate enough to acquire tickets
numbered more than five hundred and fifty persons; eager patrons swarmed
even into the Recesses and Gallery, and left enthralled by the experience.

If it is true, as has been aired about town, that the boy is
a former pupil of Haydn, as well as the grandson
of an African prince, both claims were abundantly manifest
in his lofty bearing and eloquent expression. He was presented
by his distinguished Father, who is to be commended for cultivating
a musical prodigy of so courteous and prepossessing a disposition.
One would be hard-pressed to find a more pacific and attentive
caregiver; indeed, upon completion of the Viotti Concerto
in the first half of the program, the Father, overcome by
the acclamations showered upon his progeny, wept from sheer joy.

We herald the arrival of this musical marvel to British shores
and wish him God Speed as he undertakes the London concert circuit
this winter.

Disappearance

(Kill the lights. Cut the atmo.)

A boy and his violin:
That's it. The one tucked
into the side of the other.
Both small, unremarkable—

(No no no no. Add the pink gel.)

until one of them moves:
The boy lifts his arm,
or the violin floats up
to kiss his chin.

(Spot #8 now, a whisper of gold.
Grow it and fade the pink on my count:
five four three . . . slowly, slowly.
Drown the forestage. Let it seep in.)

A man can vanish between
the downstroke and the first note's sigh,
from one word to the next, a wink and a nod.
He'll evaporate under a lady's glance
as her smile slides across the room.

(Do we want fog machines here?
A little much, maybe . . . but spill some purple
along the boards in back, then lift it
up the scrim like a rising curtain of melancholy,
an Aurora Borealis of the soul. I know,
that sucked; you get the drift.)

But a boy looks out
from the backs of his eyes.
A boy stays where you put him,
invisible, until you hiccup—
                    (Full floods, on my mark: Go!)

and suddenly he's there.

II

BREAD & BUTTER, TURBANS & CHINOISERIE

You find no man, at all intellectual, who is willing to leave London. No, Sir, when a man is tired of London, he is tired of life; for there is in London all that life can afford.

—Samuel Johnson

Hear Ye!

The Learned Pig, the Mechanical Turk, the Frenchman Tripping Over
the Plume in His Tricorner Hat—pass them by, the Season's begun!
You can't be seen slopping about the lower spectrum of open air
entertainment. Two shillings will buy you an hour of Musical Glasses
played by the delicious Miss Ford—no water in her cups,
yet they'll warble with no need of a drop! Speaking of which,

you look dry, Sir: a tuppence a tipple. Keep it moving,
that's the stuff; even if you've nowhere to get to—hurry on,
or you'll be trampled in the press. Choices! That's London:
You could follow the Janissary jingling through St. James
or stop in at Boodle's if your game is on. If you must join in,
amateur glees are sung every Friday at the Crown and Anchor,

with bawdy lyrics to follow when the ladies depart.
Feeling noble? Attend Sunday's benefit
for the castrato Tenducci, mired in debtor's prison;
Mondays are for war orphans, Tuesdays, syphilitics,
Wednesdays, for the Lying-In at Hospital in Westminster.
Got a watch? Guard the fob. Push on, past the rug beater, broom peddler,

the boy hawking pickles, the child twitching her broken tambourine.
Dodge clattering carts and trundling barrows, clacking spokes and doors
slamming on the four-in-hands heading over to Rotten Row for a highbrow
hobnob. Say what? Can't hear—what with fish hags haranguing
and unctuous urchins and flatulent hurdy-gurdies thumping out sea shanties
while rival churches toll the hours. You'd be better off examining

Charles Clagget's Ever-Tuned Organ at the King's Arms in Cornhill
or the Welsh harp at Whitehall. Failing a thirst for the exotic,
there's the orchestra at Vauxhall Gardens, oratorios at Covent Garden,
Salomon's subscription concerts in the rooms at Hanover Square.
Granted, nothing compares to the sight of Cotter the Giant
pulling a dwarf from his coat pocket (despite his size, Count Boruwlaski's

quite successful with the ladies); but if you're in the market for
condensed miracles, try the arias currently swelling Pantheon's rafters—
remarkable sonorities emanating from the tiny form of the inimitable
Madame Mara, guaranteed to snap the cords of your heart.
Smaller still? Ten-year-old Clement's always a good show, but for pure
flourish and spectacle, his rainbow opposite can be seen nightly

playing onstage at the Drury Lane Theatre: Little Mulatto Prince
George, fiddling away between Acts I and II of Handel's *Messiah*.

The Lesson: Adagio

To bow
        is to breathe: open
                  then
            fold again, slowly:
              deep inside
            a wounded angel's
            wing throbs & you
                  must find it:
                      probe
                      touch
                        heal
        In
                &
      out,
    like breathing:
                        (That's rather fine, my boy!)
Ahem:

      Out
          then
      In
        &

          Open
          Open

    wing hammering sky   ember to flame

                    Bear down
                    Feel the air
            beneath your stroke

It's your baby now   go on
                        nestle it
                        bruise it

                            make it sing

Black Pearl

London, 1790s

Pathological hit of the day: nigger on a golden chain.
Metaphorically, that is. The African
valet, the maidservant black
as aces in a hole, comely under that
there-but-for-God's-grace-go-I
hue, a negative
to her ladyship's
eggshell, blue-veined visage . . .

Who knew enhancement killed?
To achieve such alabaster,
lead-laced powders drilled
merrily into each cheek's circumference,
while the gaily upholstered
Child of the Night (aka Jigaboo)
went free of ointments,
pastes, and paint; kept her dark bloom
and smiled as she curtsied, flashed
her scalding eye.

Ode to the Moon

Diana wants to be a boy like me.
Stripped of turban, cravat, chemise:
perhaps a shirt of printed muslin
to blend in with the trees.

She is bright, she shines
like I do not. I'll be
the firmament, backdrop
to her swift-skipping knees.

She goes out in the world alone,
her quiver bouncing, pointing
right my way, at me! No—
silk's a better choice for someone

who doesn't want to be a girl
or lady, prince or beggar's son,
just needs to be let be.
A-hunting. Run, Diana, run!

Janissary Rap

See that fine thing with her wig all skyward,
primping along the Pall Mall?
I'm gonna shake my Jinglin' Johnny
till she swoons from my fare-thee-well!

> O here comes the Janissary,
> Janissary, Janissary!
> Here comes the Janissary
> dream boy band!

Ol' Prinny's hiding in Carlton House,
too fat to make the scene!
Let's swing on past the Royal Horse Guard,
and head for the Serpentine.

> O here comes the Janissary,
> Janissary, Janissary!
> Here comes the Janissary
> dream boy band!

Turbans, tunics, quilted pants,
more layers than a tipsy-cake!
Pipe and cymbal, timpani—
Come, give those epaulets a shake!

> O here comes the Janissary,
> Janissary, Janissary!
> Here comes the Janissary
> dream boy band!

Cartwheel, back flip,
buck 'n' wing;
three steps lively,
stop and sing:

> *To the right—Huh!*
> *To the left—Huh!*
> Now we're floating, now we're flowing;
> we're a river of silk!

Here comes the Janissary,
Janissary, Janissary!
Here comes the Janissary
dream boy band!

Concert at Hanover Square

June 2, 1790. George Bridgetower and
Franz Clement: child prodigies, of an age

Do not think for a moment
that we were boys. Souls
in a like anguish, perhaps;
or when in a fortunate instant
we forgot ourselves—gray mice
biting each others' tails,
rolling in the grass in our woolen knickers.

We did not understand how to covet.
We knew hatred
because we could smell it
all around us, it sang in the cool glasses
tinkling over our heads,
the carefully tended laughter,
the curious glint
of a widow's appraisal.

As for competition—ah, well.
Want was a quality I could taste,
music set my body a-roil,
I was nothing if not everything
when the music was in me.
I could be fierce, I could shred
the heads off flowers for breakfast
with my bare teeth, simply because
I deserved such loveliness.

If this was ambition, or hatred,
or envy—then I was all
those things, and so was he.

Two rag dolls set out for tea
in our smart red waistcoats,
we suffered their delight,
we did not fail our parts—
not as boys nor rivals even
but men: broken, then improperly
mended; abandoned
far beyond the province
of the innocent.

Pulling the Organ Stops

1791: St. Paul's Cathedral

[*Clement*]
Dressed for rejoicing in red jackets,
we climb the sides of the organ
to reach the knobs. I yank out a note,
mix in a fifth, an octave, add eerie flutes
and a buzzing multitude of strings.
George grins, tugging the bass flue
like a helmsman on the Thames.
I prefer the celestes, but reeds are best
for angelic trumpet blasts.

[*Bridgetower*]
It's like dancing with thunder,
scrabbling over the groaning deck
of a pitching ark to scale the mast,
Jacob climbing his ladder of light.
No reason for Franz to put on
that somber face. Look at Papa, who is—
how could he help it?—smiling
as we scoot along, poised for his nod
to release God's glory into the air.

[*Haydn*]
Understand, all music is physical.
Bassoons rattle bones; a violin tweedles
and like a tooth biting down on a sweet,

pierces the brain. But the organ
climbs into your chest, squeezing
as it shudders—a great lung
hauling its grief through the void
until we can hear how profoundly
the world has failed us.

Black Billy Waters, at His Pitch

Adelphi Theatre, 1790s

All men are beggars, white or black;
some worship gold, some peddle brass.
My only house is on my back.

I play my fiddle, I stay on track,
give my peg leg—thankee sire!—a jolly thwack;
all men are beggars, white or black.

And the plink of coin in my gunny sack
is the bittersweet music in a life of lack;
my only house is on my back.

Was a soldier once, led a failed attack
in that greener country for the Union Jack.
All men are beggars, white or black.

Crippled as a crab, sugary as sassafras:
I'm Black Billy Waters, and you can kiss my sweet ass!
My only house weighs on my back.

There he struts, like a Turkish cracker jack!
London queues for any novelty, and that's a fact.
All men are beggars, white or black.

And to this bright brown upstart, hack
among kings, one piece of advice: don't unpack.
All the home you'll own is on your back.

I'll dance for the price of a mean cognac,
Sing gay songs like a natural-born maniac;
all men are beggars, white or black.

So let's scrape the catgut clean, stack
the chords three deep! See, I'm no quack—
though my only house is on my back.
All men are beggars, white or black.

Haydn, Overheard

composing the first "London" Symphony,
No. 93 in D Major

It is a sad thing always
to be a slave,
but if slave I must, better
the oboe's clarion tyranny

than a man's cruel whims.
I stayed on at Esterháza,
writing music for the world
between spats and budgets,

with no more leave
to step outside the gates
than a prize egg-laying hen.
Even after Miklós died

and his tone-deaf son
filled the courtyard
with military parades,
I hesitated: Call it

robbing Peter to pay Paul,
but I had been homeless once
and did not care for hunger.
I was content. At times, happy:

There were commissions
sufficient to drown out
the Prince's baryton and
his demand for more

and more *divertimenti*.
My proudest thought:
that Mozart called me Friend.
My sweetest remembrance:

the black servant's child
lowering his violin to smile
and whisper (in time to the music!)
"Papa."

The strangest wages arrived from Spain
in recompense for the *Seven Last Words*
of Our Redeemer on the Cross
—a giant chocolate cake, spilling gold coins.

But the finest gift I ever received
was the vision of Johann Peter Salomon
with his flamboyant nose and cape
swirling across my doorstep:

"I've come to fetch you," he said.
It was December. We set out
from Vienna on the fifteenth
for London, that great free city.

{became free

Mrs. Papendiek's Diary (3)

The cold season passed agreeably.
We had declared the Bridgetower concert to be
our winter party and so were free of social obligations.
Evenings were spent reading, or with music
and friends—the Stowes were frequent guests,
as well as West, President of the Academy,
who would drop by with his eldest son.
Young painter Lawrence, so sorrowfully disappointed
by the Queen's rejection of his portrait,
availed himself of Mr. Papendiek's invitation
to drop in for a game of whist whenever he felt
inclined—an inclination indulged with alarming frequency,
although his burnt pencil sketches,
executed during those companionable silences
that fall after spirited conversation and good food,
were much treasured. One evening the Bridgetowers,
father and son, were enjoined to stay for cards and dinner.
Encouraged by their "shared culinary appetites,"
Mr. Papendiek unveiled his favorite fare,
sauerkraut and liver dumplings, which was well received:
The court kitchen at Esterháza would declare war over
such delicacies! exclaimed the elder Bridgetower;
everyone was amused and ate all the more.

The Dressing

Father's aside

Outside, I am not a man.
I am a thing
which in fine company
arouses awe:
that curious fusion of fear and longing
I have learned to make use of.

I am not a country
though I bear the marks
upon this countenance
of my own wretched, fragrant island
and the hopes of its enslavers
in my name: a river crossed, a conquered view.

Still, I am not that sad city. I am more
than its vainglory and collective shame.

Here, on this Isle, I am
a continent. I am so large
they cannot grasp my meaning.
Contours loom, unmapped;
my lineaments refuse coherence.
I am the Dark Interior,
that Other, mysterious and lost;
Dread Destiny, riven with vine and tuber,
satiny prowler slithering up behind
his doomed and clueless prey.

Since in their eyes I have no culture,
I am free to borrow strange adornments:
the Ottoman Sultan's quilted turban,
a French phrase, Caesar's cape
flung hyperbolically across Africa's
gaily layered robes. In this way
I have made from their lust a business.

This is their system; they understand
the service I provide—no trifling pleasure.
And if to them I am no more
than a mere phantasm,
a swarthy figment of their guilt,
yet I came to these shores yoked
to my name: Bridgetower, a reach
and a stretch—and now
I would give up my small empire
to you, my son, but not ever
must you forget that you are, indeed,
a Prince—just not the pitiable one
they worship here, not just the one
they can see.

} Bridgetower's father

The African Prince Sings Songs of Love

Guten Tag, Madame,
permit me, *s'il vous plaît* . . .
Ach, you are too kind!
C'est la musique, you understand,
quel jouissance, quel travail!
And my son, *mon petit chou,*
mój słodki chłopiec—barely ten,
this bright kernel of a boy,
Wunderkind in allen Aspekten!
Je ne sais pas—ich weiß nicht . . .
sometimes I am *betroffen*—overwhelmed—
and words fail this flooded heart.

Whereas you, *süßes Fräulein,*
you are *une lumière—excusez-moi,*
a discerning light. You see clearly
how wondrous is this music
he makes. *Mon Dieu,*
um Gotteswillen, Allah'a şükür:
There is such a thing

as beauty that hurts, *nicht wahr?*
A wound that fascinates,
dolce mordant, that aches
when you smile. Right here,
my angel. Yes there. O *ja.* Ooo la la. . . .

Abandoned, Again

Get under the sofa and go to sleep.

As if the world could be soothed
by a golden canopy,
the sagging fringe
of a day's deposits
exerting its ghostly weight.

Go! Go to sleep and—

Sleep? In this room
where your voice roughens
to her tinkling denial,
your scents commingling
(rust and cinnamon, faded rose)
into a shaggy pomander
you would force me
to hang against my heart?

stay out of my way.

No wish easier granted.
I am off, then, to anywhere.
Viotti's perhaps . . . or closer,
the royal boudoir—
the arabesques and flickering silks
of music, always music!
Only music now
can save me.

Mrs. Papendiek's Diary (4)

I don't know what to say, how to breathe—not in
all my years at court have I ever borne such a strange
series of events, such impromptu effrontery and rescue.
At the turn of the year, I had decided I would travel into town
for a few days' visit with my mother and father
as soon as the weather heartened. Finally, the first buds
freshened the roadside; I joined up with the Herschels
and together we boarded the post coach for London—
only to discover the senior Bridgetower already inside.
The Herschels balked, but it would have hardly been Christian
to disembark, so we squeezed ourselves onto a bench
and made the best of the situation. Our African impresario
kept up a merry stream of talk, which I attempted to counterpoint.
Mrs. Herschel was embarrassed and Mr. Herschel too shocked
(and worried as well, I'm sure, about the breach in social ranks)
to utter more than a choked good day; when we pulled up
to the White Horse Cellar, he seized his wife
by the elbow, doffed his hat, and scampered
before the coach had scarcely come to a standstill.

Later that evening I was beset once again by the Moor,
this time lurking in one of the dark passageways
surrounding the Palace. He asked to make
my parents' acquaintance, and when I protested
that they were too old to receive guests, asked
for a loan to fund, as he put it, "his charge's purposes."
I doubt the boy knew anything of the matter
nor would he have need of such charity; nevertheless,
I searched my purse for a guinea and a half
and resolved to forget both matter and money.

But today came the greatest tragedy: This afternoon
the very same braggart appeared at my door
with young George, asking if I would look after him
while he "tended to urgent business" in town!
"Ask" is too much a word; he simply called
the coach to stop, walked the path up to my home,
and deposited the boy.
                                    Once
his father had gone, the poor child
poured out his woes: that he was
forced to squirrel himself away
whenever his father "entertained"—
which entertainment was frequent,
and loud; that he was ashamed of the life
his father led so flagrantly and which
consequently he, as his son, must endure.

I held him to me as he wept;
I must speak to the Court about these events.

The Transaction

There are golden angels, and cockerels
        with emeralds for eyes watching everyone
who comes and who goes. A lot of that:

fans snapping shut (*swoosh-click*)
        and tap-tip-tupping of tiny
embroidered shoes

that wouldn't last a day outside
        where London is: dark birds
on the river, speckling the trash heaps.

My father's an ass
        and now he's gone.
There, I've said it.

No one whispers without purpose
        here; there's no love
in their whispers. The Prince paid for me

out of a blue velvet pouch.
        Father smirked at my speech.
The Prince has a little round belly.

(No, he doesn't. No, I didn't
        say it, say anything:
That's what I'm supposed to answer—

for the Court is vicious, far worse than
      a treacherous woman.)
I wonder where I'll sleep tonight?

The Undressing

First the sash, peacock blue.
Silk unfurling, round and round, until
I'm the India ink dotting a cold British eye.
Now I can bend to peel off my shoes,
try to hook the tasseled tips
into the emerald sails
of my satin pantaloons. Farewell,

Sir Monkey Jacket, monkey-red;
adieu shirt, tart and bright
as the lemons the Prince once
let me touch. Good-bye,
lakeside meadow, good-bye
hummingbird throat—
no more games.

I am to become a proper British
gentleman: cuffed and buckled
with breeches and a fine cravat.
But how? My tossed bed glows,
while I—I am a smudge,
a quenched wick,
a twig shrouded in snow.

Ode on a Negress Head Clock,
with Eight Tunes

Marlborough goes off to war
La da da, da da da da . . .

Whirligiggery in the key of
Grand Accidental Design:
a clock-and-music-box
inside the head of a woman.

Beneath the gilded turban,
her fat cheeks are lacquered
black; ditto the neck,
swanning sleekly up

from gleaming drapery.
But unique to this
French bit of cabinetry
is the ingenuous manner

she can be prevailed upon
to reveal her mysteries:
Tug the left earring
and the hours pop up

into her eyes; pull on the right
to start the musical engine.
For the modern ear,
however, just one song

remains: a martial ditty
about a widow waiting
for her man, who's been
shot down or speared through

but in her hopeful affections
lives on, well past Easter
and Trinity, until the loyal valet
returns in black to deliver

his tale of woe
for fifteen or more
murderous verses.
The seven other melodies

are silent—sweetly so.
We let them go; watch
as this boy, standing rapt
at the carpet's edge

(so as not to muss the fringe),
leans tentatively in to tug
the golden teardrop swinging
from her ear. Inside,

an organ winds its tiny gears,
and the widow's pink-
tinged sorrow pours
prettily into the palace room.

He shouldn't be here. (Should he?)
Her eyes can tell him nothing
but the time—the left
in Roman numerals, Arabic

the right; enameled shutters
snap apart ten minutes
to the hour. All the while,
a host of cherubs holds up

her radiant robe, wave garlands,
parade dead game upon a bier—
preoccupy themselves, in short,
with heavenly horseplay.

He gives another yank.
(It's the only tune he likes.)
Call her what you please—
exotic, incidental,

black as the sun is bright;
tomfoolery, inspired gimcrack,
or just plain thingamabob—
this doo-wop of a timepiece

charms him. What else
can a child do
with such nonsense?
(Adore it. Fear it. Whisper

Father, I'll miss you forever.)

Intermezzo

a Gavotte

Polgreen, black Polgreen,
O where have you been?

   I've been to London
   to visit the Queen.

Polgreen, dear Polgreen,
what did you do there?

   I played for the Prince
   & hid under a chair.

Tafelmusik (1)

A braised turkey shank, dressed in the paper petticoats of State,
brings water to her red mouth above the ransacked plate.
She lifts her eyes, watching him, amused—
a woman's grin, neat as a cat's. He's gotten used

to banter, but these loins of molten stone—does she know
he aches? Can she see the sheen warming his cheek,
the blush he (thank God) rarely shows?
Ever since the fish course with its delicate, unseemly reek,

he's tried humming, plotting chords . . . temptation still snakes
a hand into his lap. Who could bear to contemplate
that oozing slice of pheasant pie? Wild for any antidote,
he grabs the port, dribbles its velvet fire down his throat.

Good Lord, her lips—she's licked them.
Now they're opening, pink tongue
peeking out, stretching; then on the glistening tip
she slowly positions the snowy tit

of a meringue. Hell, he'll be hung
for a pound of flesh as well as for a morsel:
I'll climb your laced stays, milady, rung for rung;
I'll suck the marrow clean from the rib you stole.

Brothers in Spring

—*Frühling, so früh!* Ferdinand is amazed
at the onset of spring, so early in the year,

the German gutturals suddenly strange to my ears.
It's true; Spring has moved in overnight.
The garden paths are all swept yellow.

—*Just a little early*, I reply, trying for wit
(*Frühling*, literally, means "early little thing")
but he doesn't get it, smiles broadly.

Everything about him is broad—back and
shoulders, barrel chest, embarrassing thighs.

We walk as quickly as his baggage and curiosity allow,
the hem of my morning coat brushing pollen as we move along.
I must be impregnating the length of the Serpentine.

—*We call him Lenz. Lenz, for Frühling.*
Back home, Spring is a man!

I wince. Bacony blossoms wobbling eagerly
on their freshly furred stalks, musk-scent
steaming up from the lily pads: My London spring reeks.

—*Your English is good. Where did you learn it?*
An ox; a small, wine-colored ox: That's my brother.

He came hurtling off the coach, grinning at the sight of me,
then commandeered his traveling chest down from the rack,
freed the violoncello as easily as unlacing a boot.

—*You know the old man; he's obsessed with languages.*
How does one forget a brother, blood of my blood
and all that shit? But then, I barely remember our mother,

who hadn't come with us to Esterházy,
who must have stayed in Dresden to have this little snot . . .

—*How is . . . Is he . . .* (I could not help it.)
—*Gone with a wave of his cape: Poof!*
Truth be told, Mutti *and I were relieved.*

(Give me half a wing, and I'll shred the air;
a finger bone for a flute, cobwebs for my hair . . .)

The Salomon Concerts

1794

What a shame to grow up,
no longer the jigging pig.

Papa Haydn's back, and all London
is wagging tail—Salomon

leading the charge,
his stupendous nose

open, snuffling. Just
how long does he think

a half note needs to be held?
No *fermata* demands a lifetime

commitment. Look at that farmer,
sawing away at the poor violoncello

like he's thrashing rye! Easy, sir . . .
I believe you've turned over

turnips a-plenty
for your evening stew.

Another eighth note missed.
If this runaway four-in-hand

would only *listen*,
they'd feel each crescendo

as a tree feels the spring sap
surging; they'd understand

the conversation they're supposed
to be having. O torment,

thorn under the nail! Must every violist
in the Royal Society of Musicians

throb so? *Legato means
Let-it-go*, Papa used to say,

and the music will do its own singing.

Haydn Leaves London

August, 1795

I work too slowly for their appetites.
I am a plow horse, not a steed; and though
the plow horse cultivates the very grain that gilds
their substantial guts, they will thrill to any chase,
lay down a tidy fortune and their good name
on the odds of a new upstart darling.

The first trip, I took up Pleyel's unspoken dare
and promised a new piece every evening
for the length of the concert series.
Intrigue fuels the coldest ambitions;
the daily newspapers thickened
with judgments on the drummed-up duel
between the Maestro and his student of yore.
What was I thinking? I am old enough to value,
now and then, an evening spent with starlight—
not one twittering fan or lacy dewlap obscuring
my sidelong glance—yet I came back

to these noisome vapors, this fog-scalded moon,
fat and smoking, in its lonely dominion.
The black Thames pushes on. I close my eyes
and feel it, a bass string plucked at intervals,
dragging our bilge out to the turgid sea—
a drone that thrums the blood, that agitates
for more and more. . . .

                  Well, it is done.
I bore down for half a dozen occasions,
wrote a four-part canon to a faithful dog,

wheedled a few graceful tunes
from Salomon's orchestra, that bloated fraternity
of whines and whistles—and now I can return
to my drowsy Vienna, wreathed in green
and ever turning, turning just slowly enough
to keep the sun soft on her face.

Seduction Against Exterior Pilaster, Waning Gibbous

Still waters: If indeed
there were any truth
to the saying, then these
ran deeper than any
he had plumbed or wished
to enter. The deed done

quickly: almost fastidious,
the way she leaned
against the tooled stone
so he could open her,
one silvered cusp of breast
quivering as she exhaled

into the very places his hands
had found to savor.
It wasn't lust. Something
purer, an appetite *sans*
soul or mercy, rinsed clean
of the human element

he felt rising in him once more—
sweat pricking, Adam's apple convulsed
into hoarse arpeggios,
her ragged sighs lapping his ear
as, startled from a cloud,
the humpbacked moon

dumped its rapturous froth
over lawn & balustrade.
Oh. Such a tiny ecstasy for all
that trouble. His heart
pinched in the vast dark
nave of his chest.

Pretty Boy

Can't say he walked the walk.
        Talked it, but everybody
                did that, everybody
had a story to front,
        the essential mess of their life.

He was pretty, though. Nobody
        messed with the sight of him
because it messed with them
              first,
        that invisible mirror

            shining the truth
straight back. Oh he had it easy
out there
        in the world,
        promenading

his bright skin and curls,
        his agreeably knobbed nose,
        eyes black and brown lips
plush enough to sink
        a lady's dreams into
all night. . . .

        Nobody told him the truth.
Nobody had a truth worth telling
        so they talked all the time,
            no secret safe
            a week, a day, through Sunday tea—

No one could tell him anything
he really needed:
                the idea of something
precious, soothing.
He walked the length of St. James

        and kept his hankie in his sleeve;
he willed himself to smell the rot,
                powdered wigs and mud and
                dying children; he looked and looked
until he met

                one keen eye
seeing everything, too:
                        Old Black Billy Waters,
                peg leg and fiddle
        just a-going, laughing as if to say

Whatcha gonna do with that stare?
        and tossing it
                        back,
                quick as a coin
        flipped into
                a cup.

New Century Aubade

20 Eaton Street, south of Buckingham Gardens

Everything I do is a pose: one hand
gripping the balustrade, the other
cupped around a glass of air
lifted into the inked-in sky, a toast to . . .

well, who-knows-and-hell, a drunk's remorse
is mostly whimsy, anyway—
a strained revelry like this night,
wavering before the advancing forces:
Even the King's distant shrubbery grows
conspicuous, as ungainly as
a child's toys left overturned in the parlor.

No birthday for me again this year—
my odd cipher erased by court astronomers
eager to align human measure
to heavenly cadence. An awkward galopp!
But I'll dance to anything tonight,
off-kilter on my four-year-old legs;
tonight I am lit from within
by that beacon of enlightenment,
French brandy; I sway in homage
to the plumpening lawn and topiary
of your verdant realm, O
mad majesty, my dear glutted Prince!

Again! they cried, rolling in their seats
as we tuned up for the next round: *again!*
the caroling, plates clattering and flailing limbs:
again! as if the next time
would surely be the best
but not the last . . .

Pinkening sky. And with it
a small breeze
quickening, wisping my cheek,
a ghost's chill tickle . . .

Foolishness, all of it—
the lost birthdays and prodigal punch,
the extra zeroes on a clean slate—
even the bitch I walked out on
so that I could toast
this sotted stranger, my one true love
laid bare and cold before me:

hedge and meadow, castle keep.

III

STURM UND DRANG

Are all people who come to Vienna bewitched so that they have to stay here? It rather looks like it.

—Leopold Mozart

I believe that so long as the Austrian has his brown beer and sausage he will not revolt.

—Ludwig van Beethoven

The Petition

Because there comes a time.
Because there was a time.

Because I want to be known as a gentleman
everywhere.

Because Haydn came from there; came, and went back.
Because I am no longer a *Wunderkind*.

Because you saved me.

To the Continent

1803

When I was a child, I was content
to fit the notes to the joy I felt.
Chords unfurled shimmering ribbons
I twirled myself in, as if into a chrysalis.

Then I wanted love, whole sheets of it
to wrap myself warm for sleeping.
Less spontaneous, I performed vigorously;
the world was not as large as the sound

I sent to it. More admiration, fetes.
Women began sampling, nibbles & slurps;
I played to keep the noise going,
to fill me up. But now I want only

to find love that resists, notes that will not fit;
I want to be appalled & staggered
in equal measures, I want blood
& blood's aftermath—

weariness & affliction, *sans* mercy.

Old World Lullaby

I had forgotten her pinks and creams,
the sprigged apron tied on like a heavenly shield,
the small smile transfigured by the task
set before her: *Feed your sons.*

I had forgotten her nasal contralto, its feathery edges,
and the smell of old honey and almonds
whenever she moved through the kitchen—
as she does now, suddenly, to hug

then hold me at arm's length, like a wooden nutcracker,
her pale eyes searching mine, ardent for anything
I could spare, a little piece of me, a soul-scrap
tossed like bad meat to the yapping dogs in the street

Floating Requiem

Dresden, 1802–1803

Summer ended powerfully—as if God
had snapped a branch from his mightiest oak
and thundered: "Enough." The sky dimmed.
Cloaks appeared. The Elbe's blue road
turned wild and gray, struck by a grim fury.
Everywhere one trudged, stone claimed
dominion and set an implacable face
to the centuries—only to culminate
in this pleasing line of turrets and domes
along the rapidly darkening riverfront.

Wind fingered the crevices; timbered walls
stiffened as chill seeped up through our boots.
Cathedrals thrilled to their tasks: spires
bristling at twilight and the doors cranked wide
to spew out their gold.
                              High in the organ loft
we waited, my brother and I, skins burnished
by candlelight, instruments gleaming. Watched
them enter—the weary, the obedient, the curious;
a ghostly scent of malted barley rising
from their thick woolens and flaxen hair.

They came for comfort, dragging
the cold in behind them; they came for light
then closed their eyes, the better to listen:
cello ploughing low while I skimmed
the thin ice above, teased the bright edges.
All winter we played, and they lingered—
through incense and gingerbread, from Advent

to *Christkindl* to New Year's to *Drei Könige*
(a salute to Balthazar, the Dark King!)—
and when the listening was finished,
they stood up to gather their bundles,
the last candle guttered, and we stepped out
to a world rinsed of cares: A pale lemon light
shone over the river; on the far shore
I could see a faint radiance, a white path—
snowbells budding, shouldering up
through the muck for their first raw gulp
of pure ether—and I knew
it was time to take destiny
further south.

Ach, Wien

The truly great cities are never self-conscious:
They have their own music; they go about business.
London surges, Rome bubbles, Paris promenades;
Dresden stands rigid, gazes skyward, afraid.

Vienna canters in a slowly tightening spiral.
Golden façades line the avenues, ring after ring
tracing a curve as tender and maddening
as a smile on the face of a beautiful rival.

You can't escape it; everywhere's a circle.
Feel your knees bend and straighten
as you focus each step. Hum along with it;
succumb to the sway, enter the trance.

Ah, sweet scandal: No one admits it,
but we all know this dance.

Ludwig van Beethoven's Return to Vienna

Oh you men who think or say that I am malevolent, stubborn,
or misanthropic, how greatly do you wrong me. . . .
                                   —*The Heiligenstadt Testament*

Three miles from my adopted city
lies a village where I came to peace.
The world there was a calm place,
even the great Danube no more
than a pale ribbon tossed onto the landscape
by a girl's careless hand. Into this stillness

I had been ordered to recover.
The hills were gold with late summer;
my rooms were two, plus a small kitchen,
situated upstairs in the back of a cottage
at the end of the *Herrengasse*.
From my window I could see onto the courtyard
where a linden tree twined skyward—
leafy umbilicus canted toward light,
warped in the very act of yearning—
and I would feed on the sun as if that alone
would dismantle the silence around me.

At first I raged. Then music raged in me,
rising so swiftly I could not write quickly enough
to ease the roiling. I would stop
to light a lamp, and whatever I'd missed—
larks flying to nest, church bells, the shepherd's
home-toward-evening song—rushed in, and I
would rage again.

I am by nature a conflagration;
I would rather leap
than sit and be looked at.
So when my proud city spread
her gypsy skirts, I reentered,
burning towards her greater, constant light.

Call me rough, ill-tempered, slovenly—I tell you,
every tenderness I have ever known
has been nothing
but thwarted violence, an ache
so permanent and deep, the lightest touch
awakens it. . . . It is impossible

to care enough. I have returned
with a second Symphony
and 15 Piano Variations
which I've named Prometheus,
after the rogue Titan, the half-a-god
who knew the worst sin is to take
what cannot be given back.

I smile and bow, and the world is loud.
And though I dare not lean in to shout
Can't you see that I'm deaf?—
I also cannot stop listening.

First Contact

Ignaz Schuppanzigh's apartments. A musical salon.

I hear he's a wild man, a proletarian
who forgets to shave and rejects tutelage;

who'll dare nobility to trespass wherever
he decides to take his constitutionals,

but at the keyboard a wonder.
So I am exactly where I need to be,

tuning my instrument with Vienna's finest
on a sun-blown April afternoon. I've made

the rounds, Baron to Count to Prince,
had my letter of introduction passed on tray after tray

like an after-dinner drink. It's all a bit dizzying—
the lilting queries, coifed heads bobbing

in murmured goodwill; I watch late light
soften the stucco into creamy arabesques

as polite chatter swirls around me, whirls and dips
until I feel I'm being slowly stirred by a celestial

coffee spoon. At last! Schuppanzigh
moves toward the foyer, maneuvering his gut

past a mahogany secretaire and two nattering poufs
to welcome—too late!—his friend

who bursts into view, a squat invasionary force
not quite as dark as me—in coffee-speak

a *Kleiner Goldener*, Small Gold
to my Big Brown—but pocked, burly;

a dancing bear who'll refuse to entertain,
who'd ignore the yanked chain until

they slit him for a coat. He's clapping
shoulders now, shaking hands, moving forward

as the room expands, laughing. And why not?
This is his party, after all; we are here

to play *him*—this ugly, flushed little man
everyone calls "The Moor"—

although not to his face
nor, I suspect, within my earshot.

Vienna Spring

A lunatic angel has descended on Vienna!
No sooner had I given up
on the violin as no more
than a tiny, querulous beast
suited solely for dilettante monarchs
and their peg-leg street beggars,

do I make the acquaintance
of George Polgreen Brischdauer,
mulatto musician/magician most monstrous!
After such delicious execution
of an afternoon's program
so decidedly pedestrian,
there's nothing to be done but repair
to a neighboring *Wirtschaft*
where—*noch 'n Maß, Mädl!*—I fear
I must revise my former assessment:

though dipped in ink, this Jacob
has grappled the shining messenger
for a glimpse of heaven
and won the battle: Entirely master
of his instrument, he climbs the strings
agile as the monkeys from his father's land.
Ah, Immortality has a new-wrought,
human face. How I love my handsome,

brash new friend!—this twilit stranger
who has given me myself again.
So then why not everything and more,

and all at once? Four strings on a chord
with the silence beyond, solo and chorus,
the declaimed and the whispered;
all that I know and know I am losing,
have been losing,
have lost,
lost. . . .

Polgreen, Sight-Reading

Harder to play long
than fast. It's more than stretching
a line—suspension is
what we yearn for,
that delicate fulcrum between crash
and sheer evaporation, a dissipating breeze.
To levitate strands of melodic sound
across all the mired avenues
we barge along, daily—this shining wire
so light, so strong, we can just make out
(there!—there it goes) and follow,
slip note by note along
and fly—float—
in that radiant web.

Adagio sostenuto. Sustained slowness.
Not water, but the invisible current
a dove's wing skims. Not air but
the agency that stirs it.
Not light but spark—no,
the dark thread between sparks,
how your eye can read
a firefly's glimmering trail
while the rest of you is long gone,
darting leaf to leaf,
touching down

          as the piano,
          poised to intercept
          that bright cursive, descends growling,
          with a meatier
          deliquescence . . .

He frightens me. I've never heard music
like this man's, this sobbing
in the midst of triumphal chords,
such ambrosial anguish,
jigs danced on simmering coals.
Oh, I can play it well enough—hell,
I've been destined to travel these impossible
switchbacks, but it's as if I'm skating
on his heart, blood tracks
looping everywhere, incarnadine
dips and curves . . .
I'm not making sense.

You're making ultimate sense
he seems to say, nodding
his rutted, heroic brow.

Beethoven Summons His Copyist

Ferdinand Ries, May 24, 1803

As usual, nothing to transcribe
until I'm shaken out of bedclothes
and into the predawn chill:
Schnell, schnell, ich hab's!—meaning
it was in his head and I must prise it out.
I had quite given up and gone to bed,
thinking *This time he's gone too far;*
he's done in and will have to feign
ague or a cough. After all, the night before!
No—the morning of, with the concert
not midday but at 7 ante meridiem, and B.

                                in bed, propped
in a mound of blotched papers, humming.
Copy the violin part of the first Allegro quickly.
If it weren't for poor Bridgetower,
perched in the corner like an enormous crow,
fiddling the air and grinning with fear,
I'd throw down my pen and exit this madness—
genius, yes, but surely madness for any common man
to endure. . . .

                      Pale light squeezing
through the shutter-cracks washes us gray.
Even Bridgetower has transubstantiated—
ghost or vampire, hard to tell.
That's it, then. Our Blue Hour calls.
Let the devil take us if he can.

Augarten, 7 AM

Spectator One

> Heavenly, to escape the city's poisons
> and breathe honey, honey, honey!
> All praise Morning's cathedral,
> the ranks of noble linden presiding:
> May we be privileged to pass through
> their green light and feathered fragrance
> with tipped hats and mute nods,
> Amen!

The British Ambassador

> . . . There goes Schuppanzigh, huffing up the aisle
> in his entrepreneurial trappings.
> Dear God, the man expands weekly!
> Ah, the Archduke. And Prince Lobkowitz,
> poor soul . . . such an unsightly specimen
> and feels just as miserable as he looks.
> I'd have ended it years ago, gone out like a man.

Spectator Two

> Curious beginning—solo violin,
> reminiscent of Bach but wilder, a supplication—
> and the piano's reply is almost a lover's,
> a bird on a cliff returning its true mate's call.

Child

　　　　He moves around too much.
　　　　He's like a poplar in the wind!

Spectator Three

　　　　For a savage he plays quite nicely.
　　　　As for his figure—tall, slim,
　　　　dare I say elegant? I'd heard
　　　　he was a charmer, but never thought
　　　　chimney soot applied to countenance
　　　　could be considered handsome.

Spectator Two

　　　　What a furious storm he rides!
　　　　And Beethoven listing side to side
　　　　in accord with the gale,
　　　　bobbing that Rumpelstiltskin head
　　　　as if to say "Well done, my boy." . . .
　　　　That's it—a father to his prodigal son,
　　　　come home at last.

British Ambassador

> To call this a sonata is obscene.
> A Presto is presto and Adagio . . .
> well, slow is meant to stay slow.
> This Beethoven is as loopy as they say—
> imagine, insulting the Prince
> when he simply requested a song,
> smashing figurines, dashing off
> in the middle of dinner!

Spectator One

> I thought that infernal back-and-forth
> would never cease. A concert's meant
> for reverie, to drift away
> on nature's curative susurrations . . .
> ah, a Theme and Variations—
> that's more like it.

Child

> I like his waistcoat.
> How can he see out
> from all that darkness?

The Performer

Adagio sostenuto / Presto / Tempo primo

> I step out.
> I step out into silence.
> I step out to take
> my place; my place is silence
> before I lift the bow and draw
> a fingerwidth of ache upon the air.
> This is what it is like
>
> to be a flame: furious
> but without weight, breeze
> sharpening into wind, a bright gust
> that will blind, flatten all of you—
> yet tender,
> somewhere inside
> tender. If you could see me
>
> now, Father, you would cry—though
> you wept easily, as I remember,
> and even so it was manly,
> the way that thick black fist
> daubed your cheek
> with those extravagant sleeves
> quivering.
>   I prefer to stand,

cheek cushioned, and soothe her
as I pull the sobs out,
gently . . . yes, you hear it.
You who made me can hear it—
just as he's making me
hear it now, so that I can
pull it from her.

Andante con Variazioni

Thank you. It was a privilege. You are so kind.
It is all his doing; I am merely the instrument.
To have the honor of this première . . .
a beauty of a piece, indeed.

What an honor! Countess, I am enchanted.
I only wish I could better express my gratitude
in your lovely language: *Vielen Dank*.
It is all his—why, thank you, sir. I am speechless.

Gern geschehen, Madame; did I say that correctly?
(God I sound like my father.)
I believe he is pleased. I sincerely hope so . . .
but you are kindness incarnate. No, my privilege entirely.

Herr van Beethoven is indeed a Master, and Wien
an empress of a city. My apologies—
I only meant that she is . . . magnificent.
(Ludwig, get me out of here!)

Finale

If this world could stop
for a moment
and see me;
if I could step out
into the street and become
one of them,
one of anything,
I would sing—
no, weep right here—to simply
be and be and be . . .

VOLKSTHEATER

A Short Play for the Common Man

Georgie Porgie,
or
A Moor in Vienna

CAST OF CHARACTERS (& I mean characters!)

GEORGE AUGUSTUS POLGREEN BRIDGETOWER, celebrity violinist
LUDWIG VAN BEETHOVEN, composer
SCHUPPANZIGH, director of the Augarten concerts
FERDINAND RIES, Beethoven's copyist
TUSSI, a barmaid

CHORUS OF BAD GIRLS
The usual collection of gawking spectators, drunken clientele, &
general riffraff

Scene One: Outside the Augarten

(SCHUPPANZIGH *enters stage left, clapping* F. RIES *heartily on the shoulder,
causing* RIES—*a none-too-hearty young man—to wince repeatedly.*)

SCHUPPANZIGH: Well now, Ries, what d'you say to that?
                 Never thought it'd come together that swiftly, eh?
                 A *tour de force*, no less than a *tour de force*, I'd say!

RIES: (*muttering*)   Yes, you would say that.

SCHUPPANZIGH: What? What was that?

RIES: I said: I'd dare say you're right!

SCHUPPANZIGH: You'd say I say?
What kind of gibberish are you sputtering, lad?
That's the problem with you young acolytes
of Master B—you're half addled yourself,
keeping up with his rages,
picking up scribbled pages stained
with the grease from a half-eaten schnitzel . . .
Had you running all night, did he? What a scene
that must have been—crazy as a hen house!

RIES: (*muttering*) You could say that.

SCHUPPANZIGH: What? Speak up, boy!

RIES: (*with dignity*) I wasn't worried.

SCHUPPANZIGH: 'Course not, 'course not, my lad.
He's a genius, after all.

(*Shouting.*)

Ludwig! My dear Ludwig—
put a move on, why don't you?
There's celebrating to be done!

(*Enter* BEETHOVEN, *ascot unloosed, with his arm awkwardly draped
around* GEORGE BRIDGETOWER, *who is several inches taller.*)

SCHUPPANZIGH: Hey-o, boy-o! Big B and little b!
I see you brought along your shadow.

RIES: Which is which?

SCHUPPANZIGH: What's that you say, boy-o?
Why don't you speak up?

BEETHOVEN: (*bellowing*)
        Watch it, Ries! I can read lips!

SCHUPPANZIGH: A man and his shadow!
        You have *Schattenfieber,* milord!

BRIDGETOWER: Whereas I stay cool.

        (*All freeze and look at him, dumbfounded, as if
        a palm tree had suddenly spoken.*)

BRIDGETOWER: German, anyone?

        (*then loudly, signifying*)

        I got it made in the shade!

        (*He does a little fraternity stepping. The others relax,
        visibly relieved: This is how he's supposed to act.*)

BEETHOVEN: Hmmph.

(*Staggers backward to observe the dance.* RIES *catches him as he reels; he
bounces back and is propelled forward into* BRIDGETOWER'*s open arms.*)

BRIDGETOWER: What th—?

BEETHOVEN: *Mein lieber Bursch!*

RIES: (*muttering*)   You've said that already.

SCHUPPANZIGH: Yes, indeedy—and in front of the entire
        gossip-mongering, chocolate-sipping
        populace of Vienna! Now they've got
        even more to sniff at besides their snuff!

BEETHOVEN: (*arms around* BRIDGETOWER, *blubbering*)
Mein Sohn! Mein Sohn!

SCHUPPANZIGH: Speak English, Ludwig!
The boy can't understand you.

BRIDGETOWER: Oh, but I can! My mother is half Polish,
half German; and my real father—

(*glancing at* BEETHOVEN)

spoke seven languages:

(*ticking them off on his fingers*)

English, German, French, Hungarian, Arabic . . .

RIES: (*muttering*) Yes, yes, we get the drift.

BEETHOVEN: Speak up, Ries! You stepped in shit?

SCHUPPANZIGH: (*under his breath*)
Scheisse.

BEETHOVEN: I can read your lips, Schuppi!
Hell, I can read your mind!

SCHUPPANZIGH: What am I thinking, then?

(*A trenchant pause. All pose, as in a Marx Brothers tableau.*)

BEETHOVEN: That . . . that it's time for another Stein!

ALL: (*exeunt, singing*)
Beer here, beer here!
Or we'll all fall down—*juchhe!*

Scene Two: En Route

(*Still singing,* BEETHOVEN, SCHUPPANZIGH, RIES, *and* BRIDGETOWER *enter, joined by a few* BAD GIRLS.)

BAD GIRLS & COMPANY:
Off to The Black Camel we go, heigh-ho!
Its wines are quite learnéd
and legendary;
from spice house to restaurant,
with clientele *trés galant,*
three cheers for that famed sunburned
dromedary!

(*A triumvirate of white-robed maidens appears; the one in the middle carries a large scroll with golden tassels.*)

THE TRIO:
Hold it right there!

BAD GIRL #1:
Who are you?

THE TRIO:
The handmaidens of Kronos.
We oversee the accurate chronicling of events.

BAD GIRL #2:
Come again?

LEFT-HAND MAIDEN:
We manage time.
You're out of sync.

BAD GIRL #1:
Oh. (*shrugs*) So?

RIGHT-HAND MAIDEN: (*impatiently*)
So you can't go to "The Black Camel"
because you don't know about it yet!

HEAD MAIDEN: According to our records . . .

(unscrolls a lengthy, impressive parchment; peering through a lorgnette)

"Zum schwarzen Kameel" was established as a spice and exotic foods shop in 1618—

BAD GIRL #2:   —See!!

HEAD MAIDEN: *(casting a withering glance; continuing)*
                —by the merchant Johann Baptist Cameel
                in Bognerstrasse 5. A tavern was added
                in the early nineteenth century; however,
                (a warning glance again, pointedly)
                one must remember two things:
                Number 1, the Wirtshaus was not located
                in the heart of Vienna at that time,
                but in the country resort of Mödling;
                Number 2, Ludwig van Beethoven did not begin
                frequenting the locale until 1818, when
                he spent the first of three summers there
                upon the recommendation of his doctors,
                who had prescribed the Mödling baths
                presumably as a palliative to hearing loss.
                With the aid of his sketchbook
                Beethoven would take quiet walks—

RIES: Real quiet!

(He gets nudged by a gum-popping BAD GIRL.)

HEAD MAIDEN: —in the surrounding woods, and there
                found inspiration for *Missa Solemnis*—

BAD GIRL #1:   Okay, okay, we get your point.

HEAD MAIDEN: —and the Ninth Symphony . . .

SCHUPPANZIGH: Geez, he'll write nine of them?

RIGHT-HAND MAIDEN:
Our point, wretched mortals, is that you are firmly lodged in the year 1803. He hasn't even finished the Third Symphony, much less torn up the dedication page to Napoleon . . . oops!

(*She claps her hand over her mouth, as the chief handmaiden nudges her sharply. An embarrassed silence as all turn to look at* BEETHOVEN—*who, as fate would have it, appears not to have heard; he's been leaning against a tree the entire time, with* BRIDGETOWER *whispering urgently into his deaf ear.*)

HEAD MAIDEN: (*attempting to make light of the error; loftily*)
This stays between us, *nicht wahr?*

ALL: (*muttering*) *Ja, ja. Wahr, wahr.*

(THE HANDMAIDENS OF KRONOS *turn and exeunt in a cloud of golden dust, which sends* RIES *into a coughing fit. He's led off by one of the* BAD GIRLS, *who claps him on the back as he gazes gratefully down her décolleté; she already has a hand in his back pocket.*)

SCHUPPANZIGH: (*timidly*)
So I guess it's the Prater?

(*All nod. A pause; then, they break out into song and revelry as they exeunt, stage left.*)

COMPANY: To the Prater! To the Prater!
If you ain't been there, you oughter!
There a girl, after you've caught 'er
will make you spill your holy water!

Scene Three: The Prater

(The Prater: Vienna's fabled amusement park, where aristocracy rubs elbows with the lower classes. BEETHOVEN & COMPANY *are seated inside one of the many wine taverns that line the midway. From the array of mugs and the amount of spilled beer soaking the sawdust under their table, we can assume they've been drinking for quite some time.)*

BRIDGETOWER: *Hallo,* Dirndl! *Noch 'n Maß!*

BEETHOVEN: Don't call her that! She has a name, you know.

BRIDGETOWER: Oh yeah?

(The barmaid approaches, prettily blonde.)

What's your name, darling?

BARMAID: *(blushing)* Oh never you mind, sir.
          'Tis of no importance.

BEETHOVEN: *(stands and all but clicks his heels as he extends his hand)*
          Oh, but it is, I assure you.
          My name is Ludwig van Beethoven.

BARMAID: *(amazed, backing away somewhat)*
          My goodness!

BRIDGETOWER: *(jumping up, actually clicking his heels—as the others snigger—and extending his hand with a smile calculated to melt ice)*
          Oh, but I beg to differ, mademoiselle.
          Everything about you is important.

(Mesmerized, she extends her hand across the table. BEETHOVEN *kisses it gently, honorably; then looks on imploringly as* BRIDGETOWER *turns her hand over, kisses the palm, closes her fingers around it.)*

BRIDGETOWER: Keep that some place safe, won't you?

(She curtsies, blushing, and skitters off. The company
explodes in laughter.)

SCHUPPANZIGH: *(clapping* BRIDGETOWER *on the shoulder)*
Brilliant, B-Boy, bloody brilliant!

BAD GIRL #1:   I ain't never seen anything so smooth.

BAD GIRL #2:   I got something he could hold safe anytime!
(giggles)

BEETHOVEN: We shouldn't toy with her. She's . . . different.

BAD GIRL #2:   Oh, yeah? How so?

BEETHOVEN: I don't know. Different.

(nearly whispering it)

Noble.

BRIDGETOWER: I bet anyone here a Thaler
I can make her flip that skirt of hers
with a snap of my fingers!

SCHUPPANZIGH & BAD GIRLS:
You're on, Georgie.

SCHUPPANZIGH: Where'd you learn to schmooze like that, boy?

BRIDGETOWER: From my father: Friedrich Augustus Bridgetower,
valet to Miklós the Magnificent, of Esterházy power,
self-proclaimed African Prince and ladies' man
extraordinaire.

He re-imagined himself with a Turkish flair
and became my first promoter. From him I learned
how to make 'em blush, how to make 'em burn.

SCHUPPANZIGH: (*snickers to himself*)
In this case, Moor is certainly more!

BRIDGETOWER: But I'm a natural man, born under a magical caul,
I'm that last plump raisin in the cereal bowl;
I'm the gravy you lick from your mashed potatoes,
I'm creamier than chocolate, juicier than ripe tomatoes!
I'm older than the ages, yet younger than a minute;
I'll parade on a pinhead or waltz upon a spinet.
I strung an empty coconut and fiddled
my way out of burning Rome—

You thought young Nero done it?
No—'twas yours truly, yours alone.
Hell, if I'd been Oedipus, old Jocasta
would've stayed alive just to call me her masta!

Y'all just sit back and watch me work.
This Dirndl will soon be minus a skirt.

(*The* BARMAID *returns with a circlet of giant beer mugs in each hand.
She squats slightly in order to deposit the mugs on the table
without spilling a drop.*)

SCHUPPANZIGH: *Hoppla!* You've given us some
heavenly head . . . on the beer, I mean!

(*Guffaws.* BEETHOVEN *glares.*)

BRIDGETOWER: Mademoiselle?

BARMAID: Yes sir?

BRIDGETOWER: Do you still have it?

BARMAID: What, milord?

BRIDGETOWER: My kiss. I told you to keep it safe.

BAD GIRL #2:   I got a key you can turn anytime, chocolate drop!

BEETHOVEN: Don't do this, Polgreen.

BRIDGETOWER: And your name? My friend here
                 asked your name, but you did not give it.
                 You did not deem us worthy, I dare say.

BARMAID: It's . . . Tussi, sir.

BRIDGETOWER: Lovely. Please—call me George.

BARMAID: Yes si—George.

BRIDGETOWER: (*politely*)
                 The kiss?

BARMAID: (*opening her palm*)
                 It's . . . here.

BRIDGETOWER: I'll let you in on a little secret:
                 A black man's kiss is a dangerous item
                 and must be handled prudently. (*pointing to her palm*)
                 Now that kiss there will hold its potency
                 for a good little while. For about of week,
                 I wager, you can place that little palm of yours
                 anywhere on your person and feel
                 my lips there. Or—

                 (*leaning in*)

you could
sample the whole article tonight.
What time do you get off . . . work?

BARMAID: (*whispering, fist clenched to her heart*)
Seven o'clock. (*pause*) George.

BRIDGETOWER: Ah! Lucky number seven. Lucky for me.

(*He kisses her cheek, lingering. She stares at him, then runs off.*
BRIDGETOWER *sits down in the silence.*)

BAD GIRL #1:   God DAMN.

BAD GIRL #2:   That other black dude's got nothing on him!

SCHUPPANZIGH: What other black dude?

BAD GIRL #2:   You know, what's his name—
had the white girl on her knees
and then strangled the bitch?

SCHUPPANZIGH: Othello! That's it—
you're our own dear Othello!
Othellerl in Vienna!

(*sings*)

"*Wien, Wien, nur du allein . . .*"

BAD GIRL CHORUS: (*singing to the tune of* "My Boyfriend's Back")
Othello's back and there's gonna be a ruckus:
Hey Viennese, Othello's back!
He'll grab your Hooters girl and shout:
Come here gal, and pluck us!
Hey Viennese, Othello's back!

Oy, the violin's his only training.
Boy, his *Wortschatz* needs explaining!

Did you hear the one about—
No, but if you hum a few bars, I bet
He'll play it anyway! *Dum, dum dum* . . .

BEETHOVEN: (*interrupting, jumping up*)
Intolerable! I can't . . . I won't . . .

SCHUPPANZIGH: What's with you, big boy?

BEETHOVEN: Womanhood is not to be treated like . . . trash!
This is an abomination! You are an abomination!

BRIDGETOWER: Hold on there, Wiggerl.
We're just having a little fun—

BEETHOVEN: Don't Wiggerl me! You heathen, you . . . savage!

(*Stomps off. A shocked silence; then the* COMPANY *erupts in confusion.*)

SCHUPPANZIGH: Hey, Wiggi, my man!
I say, Beethoven—wait up!

(*Exits, others following.*)

(*Meanwhile, it seems that* BEETHOVEN *has reconsidered;
he charges into the bar again.*)

BEETHOVEN: She was a goddess, a Queen,
And would've fled this rude scene
If she'd only been given a chance.
Such pale hair and green eyes!—
What a suitable prize
For a German dead-set on romance.

I have written about her
In my Moonlight Sonata—
Though her name was another's, who cares?
Upon crossing God's portal
True love turns immortal,
Transformed into heavenly airs!

(*The* COMPANY *stumbles back into the tavern, out of breath.* BEETHOVEN
wheels on them, waving his copy of the Violin Concerto in their faces.)

BEETHOVEN: Philistines! Snickering at honest emotion,
                     trampling on genius with your—

                     (*glancing at their shoes*)

                     muddy heels!

BRIDGETOWER: Listen up, Maestro:
                     If I said something to offend you,
                     I apologize from the depths of my—

BEETHOVEN: See? You don't even *know* what you did wrong!

                     (*thrashing* BRIDGETOWER *with the concerto as he
                     quotes the dedication from memory*)

                     "Mulatto Sonata, composed
                     for the mulatto Bridgetower,
                     great lunatic and mulatto composer."
                     Yes, lunatic—and great in no way
                     but the most vile!

                     (*Gives him a final slap with the score.*)

                     I challenge you, sir!

BRIDGETOWER: Back it up, man. This goes too far—

BEETHOVEN: Just as I suspected:
                 The monkey is nothing but a chicken.

                 (*raising the manuscript above his head*)

                 Now you will taste the high price
                 of my affection—"Mulatto Sonata," indeed!
                 I would sooner dedicate my music
                 to a barnyard mule.

(*He tears the dedication page to shreds. A collective gasp as* BEETHOVEN
        storms out. Silence for a beat, then:)

BAR GIRL #1:   *Hoppla.*

IV

"ALL IS ASHES"

This Kreutzer is a good dear fellow who gave me much enjoyment when he was here—his modesty and his natural ways appeal to me much more than all the *exterieur* or *inferieur* of most virtuosos. Since the Sonata was written for a competent violinist, the dedication to him is all the more appropriate.

—Beethoven to Nikolaus Simrock, Bonn, October 14, 1804

Beethoven does not understand the violin.

—Rudolphe Kreutzer

Tail Tucked

Not much left to do
but pay your respects
—bow, genuflect?—
to the ochre façades of a city
you'd wanted to conquer . . .

no, make that seduce.
Well, what of it? Turns out
the Grand Old Man
has a temper, plus some
addled idea of honor

that overblown barmaid
wouldn't have known
what to do with
if it had slapped her
on her extraordinary ass.

Vorsicht: Forget
the Dirndl. She's a picked bone.
And hadn't the Old Fart
leapt up from the keyboard
to embrace you

in front of everyone?
Mein lieber Bursch,
everyone listening, isn't that
what he had called you?
Time to leave

this tiered confection
of a city, this coquette
who pretends to sip
then slings the rest away,
who has spit you out

like coffee dregs. . . .
Why, they're quit of me—
they've rinsed the cup.
As if on cue,
it begins to rain.

Rain

Vienna, June 1803

Silver ribbons stripped loose from their implacable
eyelets, fingers stuttering through muffled lace,
skittering from the keyboard in disgrace.

Whimpered accompaniment to a tongued nipple.
Cascade-glimmer of a chromatic scale.
Tiny bone clack against porcelain, roast squab

or dove dripping from china plates; a sweating pail
of ice, kicked over by a horse. *Ach*, to be robbed
in one's sleep, robbed between a sip and a laugh!

(Because we're wading through wreckage, we're
not even listening to all the crash and clatter—
chords wrenched from their moorings, smashed
etudes, arpeggios glistening as they heave and sink.)

Ciphers, the lot of them. Their money, their perfumed stink.

Esterháza, Prodigal

Then he saith, I will return into my house from whence I came out;
and when he is come, he findeth it empty, swept, and garnished.
                                                                —*Matthew 12:44*

1.

What remains? Not much.
Gilt, and columns he recognizes
as Ionic, cool shafts of white cloud
peeling now, the dark oak rotting
beneath.
                    (To a boy it was
            sheer phantasmagoria,
            mystery's faint perfume;
            glimmering gowns, fans set aflutter
            by invisible feminine engines,
            and the chimney sweep surveying us
            from his corner, quiet watchfulness
            under a hooded eye.
            I saw the gridwork of power
            and thought it was Delight.)

Esterháza, the Hungarian Versailles.

2.

Heat, of course. It grew a steady crop of dulling
from May until Guy Fawkes embers cooled;
not pleasant, a heat that declared
Enemy and a foreign occupation in invisible march
sweeping bats up from the hay bales
on the road to Széplak,

a black lace unfurling
        against the molten scrim
                of day's end . . .

        (The puppet theater was my favorite
        hiding place, dark and glimmering,
        a cave inside
        a treasure chest. I sang to myself.
        It was like being buried in jewels.)

3.

Silence where once there were ceaseless
operas, banquets, shooting parties;
fancy-dress balls at the end of which
the aristocracy would repair to assorted terraces
to watch the domestics and villagers
treated to food and drink.

        Along the roadside
        booths, magicians:
        To observe common folk
        in their Sunday Best
        considered the culmination
        of festivities, a welcome
        "amusement."

4.

Steps chipped and sagging where the revelers climbed them.
The footmen in maroon, gloved, bowing.

What a majestic blood bath,
complete with epaulets
adrift in golden froth!

(on the road
dwarf Johann,
weeping,
tiny
under his bulging pack)

5.

Barbiere di Siviglia.
Paisiello's *L'amor contrastato.*
Cimarosa's *Il credulo* and *L'impresario in angustie.*
Thwarted Love. The Dupe.
The Manager in Distress.

Who needs a fortune-teller
when there's a libretto around?

6.

My life in title pages (Gothic script).

Home Again

July 1803

We have played our concerts here.
(I am finished.) Why drum up
more opportunities to be fawned over?
I am done with this "concertizing."
(Brother, do not smirk. Gloating does not become you.)

Forgive me, Mother. The trip has addled
my manners. Vienna was . . . exhausting.
(Circles within circles.) Oh, beautiful
too, of course, but rather too falsely animated.
(Arrogant swill, with their Archdukes and sandstone palisades.)

Yes, "pretentious" is the word.
(I am a fool. I have lost it all.)

He was great. Is great.
He hadn't finished the score and the copyist
nearly lost his wits scribbling madly
the night before.
                    My part?

Oh, portions were illegible,
but I didn't mind. I understood him.
I merely listened, and followed.
He frightened me, but I followed.

The concert was a sensation. I was feted.
We went out on the town.
(Weren't we comrades? True brothers,
who can drink and curse the night through

yet swear loyalty all the more fiercely
come morning?)
                    Yes, the gardens were splendid.
Being further south, summer was already upon us
and everything brimmed with color; you could say
(yes, brother, say it) the blooms were flamboyant
to the point of insolence, almost unbearable
in their profusion.
                    Oh, I'm babbling.
Pay me no mind.

Eroica

Beethoven at Castle Jezeri, Bohemia

A room is safe harbor. No treachery creaks the stair.
I've locked the door; I will not hear them knocking.
Anyone come calling can call themselves blue.

There was a time I liked nothing more than walking
the woods above Vienna, tramping forest paths
to find a patch of green laid square and plush.

I'd sit, tucked in a tapestry of birdsong, and wait
for my breath to settle; let the sun burnish my skin until
the winged horn of the post coach summoned me home.

And then everything began to sound like
the distant post horn's gleaming trail. . . .

I was careless then, I squandered the world's utterance.
And when my muddy conspirator swayed and quaked
like the tallest poplar tossed by the lightest wind

so that I could *read* his playing, see my score
transcribed on the air, on the breeze—I breathed
his soul through my own fingers and gave up

trying to listen; I watched him and felt
the music—it was better than listening,
it was the last pure sound . . .

(My emperor, emptied of honor,
has crowned himself with gold.)

Why did that savage say it? Why did I hear
what he said, why did I mind what I heard?
Good days, bad days, screech and whistle:

Sometimes I lay my head on the piano
to feel the wood breathing, the ivory sigh.
I know Lichnowski listens some evenings;

he climbs the four flights and hunkers on
the stoop. Odd: I can hear his wheezing
and not this page as it rips—the splitting

so faint a crackle, it could be the last
embers shifting in the grate. . . .

Tafelmusik (2)

Style and flattery will get you the life
you deserve: one table setting after another,
beer and cards in the park at Ranelagh,
some lame poet enthusing over
the pale moon under the pricking stars
while Lord Petersham glimpses himself
in the sheen of his boots and smiles
as he pulls out the snuffbox for this very day.
At least the unnamed gentleman who
each evening squires a different doll
from his own bisque collection
knows that's all he wants.

Does all that powder make them happier?
There's the Duchess of Devonshire, snooting past
with her lap dog, as big a yawn as ever.
Look at sly little Miss Lady Wilson prattling on;
she's absolutely *smitten* with the divertimento!
Smitten: as if this were a love affair
and she needs to be hit between the eyes
to actually *feel* something. Divertimenti
do not smite: only God does.

Here's a modest proposal: Shut your eyes
for five minutes and listen. Easy music,
yet it demonstrates respectable employment
of chordal modulation and is utterly
capable of transporting a weary soul

out of this frenzy and onto the plain
of perfect comprehension—and there is
your bliss, flowing beneath all the fretting;
there is your ecstasy & ruin & entitlement,
all the religion you'll ever need.

The Countess Shares Confidences over *Karneval* Chocolate

He was a stormy pedagogue,
always interrupting the prettiest airs—
even his own compositions,
which I was given to understand
he did not permit everyone to play.
I pounced upon each chord
with the ignorant ardor of youth;
I was sixteen, after all, and he was already
famous in Vienna, where such
approbations are stingily accorded.

He insisted on a light touch. He himself
was a wild man, ripping the music
from my stumbling fingers
and stomping about as the pages
fluttered sadly earthwards,
like the poor pheasants dropped over
the hunting fields of the *Prater*.
Rest assured I soon learned to play
more lightly! He was pleased, then,
and a quick soft smile would crimp

that dismal chunk of a face,
a sight just slightly less repugnant
than his rages. He was exceedingly
unlovely, yes, but with a threadbare
elegance—much as a servant,
envisioning gentility, might
avail himself of the scraps and dashes

from the milliner's basket.
Sometimes I could coax him
to the pianoforte, where

he would bow his head,
eyes closed, and wait—
as if the silence spoke only to him;
before playing without notes
music of such inexpressible beauty,
I thought to breathe and disturb the air
would break his heart. He would not
consent to payment, but accepted the linens
I had sent up to his rooms. Poor man—
he thought I had sewn them myself.

Andante con Variazioni

Base level's this: A day like all others,
blessed with sun, or not . . . the heart's
in place, for once. Occasionally
the world offers a kindness, and I return
the favor. Ecstasy for these small services—
the proper temperature of tea, the cream introduced
tenderly. Fair enough, that.

So I'm content. As in: comforted by
the mere presence of a heartbeat.
For once not aglow with performance,
nor dingy with standing out.

Var. I.

Sun's out, and all the tender ladies are in light cloth, frills buoyant
on bosoms, each flippant tit (that's what they are, you bitches)
an accent or grace note, if you will, to . . . well, I won't offend.
Not even in thought; I must behave the *proper gentleman*.
After all, I'll not forget what I saw at the traveling fair
my companion sought to shield from me: two monkeys
in identical red waistcoats, one with a toy violin . . .

Var. II.

The game is played with the eyes—quick flicks
when the hand is languid, lifting the lady's
to kiss, but when the arm whips out in the flare of
a proper and deep bowstroke . . . that's when to look up
and linger. We attend to table, our banter a cover,
storm high in the trees: each delicacy noted, tasted,
eyes bobbing safely above neckline while the words—
ah trippingly, sir, trippingly.

Var. III. Minore

My bed is a curse to me, it reeks of dreams,
darkness complete. The city thuds on—
clangs, bells, whipcrack and whinny,
the swishing grunts of the poor scampering for curfew;

I can hear the straw under their weary limbs.
I can hear this silence, too, silence I'm meant to fill
with chatter, obsequies, and O Lord music . . .
I do think music is a grace but it is as well
the eye of God—baleful,
glittery with his glorious outrage.
Not mine. Not mine. Give me a ball
and I will bounce it before you,
masters. Glorious in my red coat.

Var. IV. Maggiore

I'd pluck an eye out. Let it roll cobble to cobble
like a pebble tumbling, kicked up by a coach run too fast.

I pluck my string instead and it is a light sound, dilettante.
I do not like the tease of a string engaged so curtly.
Picked at. But that long breath of a bow
drawn across it, that feathered sigh swelling to a moan,
to ecstasy—no bird nor mammal utters thus.
Arco. It is a human cry, a susurration that compels the blood
to spill for a sunset or a delicious pair of eyes, an elfin ankle.

Why do I throb so unseemly? I am not a prince
of anything but darkness. I must settle my humors.
When I go for a stroll and happenstance takes me
inevitably to the Thames, there
I can stand and watch the ashen waters
rippling the boaters' oars, and I feel
for hours afterwards
a sustenance. That is the story

I wish to read, the line of song I'd follow into thin air. . . .

Haydn Serenades the Napoleonic Honor Guard

Vienna, May 1809

When I was a boy, I snipped off
a choirmate's pigtail
just to see if the scissors were sharp.
I was caned, then expelled.
I had no prospects.
My voice had cracked.
The streets were cold and lacked music.

And now you have arrayed yourselves
into a thorny hedge around my home.
You have been placed in the streets
by a pugnacious little man
who has learned to stomp his foot
until the continent quakes.
I am weary of his chronic percussion.
My emperor has fled; across the city
rooftops are breaking out with white flags
like pustules blotching a beloved face.

I have never been good-looking
but have always dressed carefully.
Now that I am old, your leader
wants to keep me safe. Spare me
your crude fanfare, Honor Guard!
I have starved in these streets with nothing
but a splintered voice
and the angels inside my head,

found Paradise while dozing
before the sparse embers
in an old friend's only grate,
the warm milk thick on my tongue;
even now it is the grandest
taste I have known.

In the end, it was a good thing
to have had no influences;
every day now for as many days as are given me
I will rise and dress, and go to the clavier
to play my folk song, my final oratorio
so those who need to will hear.

Admit it, toy soldiers
in your fine blue and gold trappings,
your white-strapped chests:
Even your ears are humming,
even your red plumes shake.

The Regency Fete

1811: The Prince Regent celebrates himself

I have always believed that love is
an overflowing, an abundance one needs
to be rid of, to pour into another. That other
can be a man or a woman, dog or hillock
or headdress of ostrich feathers; it can be
sculpture or shoreline or even a sunless day
seeping its silvery light over the Thames.
It may arrive quietly, a moment between moments
in the river of talk, after the hot soup but before
the mutton; or it can be the mutton, too—
its ginger tang and musky finish.
However it comes, the sensation is
massive, inconvenient, undeniable.

If one were to banish extravagance,
all longing would take on edges. Witness
the general, poised on the smoking field,
as he surveys the strewn body bits
with a ghoulish mix of rue and relish;
he has won another snippet of territory
and is hungry for more. Love is rounder
and less dignified; if love brandished a sword
I would kneel and bare my neck.

Some call me gaudy, capricious; it's true
that I drool when I drink and cannot walk the path
from bed to breakfast tray without wheezing.
I'm gouty, corseted, flatulent—but it's all
because I cannot refuse a thing its chance
to shine, to sigh or deliquesce. So let there be

stars in every glass and fireworks over the park,
spun sugar pagodas on mirrored lakes, diamonds,
a footman in ancient armor, crimson drapery;
and down the center of the banquet table
set for two hundred in the Gothic conservatory

an actual stream—pure water cascading
between banks of real moss with tiny flowers—
and fish flashing, gold and silver, down the sluice.

More pineapples, more cherry wine!
Tell the other two thousand guests
gathered in Carlton House
that we are here to show the world
England's swaggering heart;
and that I intend to celebrate all century,
until something even grander arrives—
more outrageous and beautiful—to swallow me
in its monstrous, invisible embrace.

Cambridge, Great St. Mary's Church

I kneel, but not in sufferance,
not in faith. There is a fulcrum
beyond which the bow tip wobbles;

no ardency nor forceful wrist
can make it sing. I am there,
at wit's balancing point. Music

pours through the blackened nave,
hollowing my bones to fit
the space it needs. It needs

so much of me, the soul's
wicked cartridge emptying
as fast as it fills. I kneel

because even the reed bends
before God's laughter
splits it, and the storm

moves on.

Panopticon

Carlton House, London, 1812

Music played for the soul is sheer pleasure;
to play merely for pleasure is nothing
but work. Is anyone listening? I am
the First Violinist of the Prince Regent's

Prized Private Orchestra, playing
for your satisfaction—except
His Mad Majesty's son is a gluttonous fool,
and I'm as invisible as a statue of a moor.

Laughter drifts between the staves
like sunlight through the iron-black pikes
of Windsor's Middle Ward, back
when I was beginning: the courtyard

a blazing field of chipped stones
combed into swirls, like the yellow dust
at Esterházy: matted down, awaiting
the guests' arrival . . . everything

done for the pleasure of others,
so they might exclaim *All this*
for me? Such extravagance!—
as it unrolled beneath their dainty steps.

Stop bitching: There's worse work
and crueler wardens. In the end,
each note sent pearling
over their dull heads

is mine—although they believe
they own it all, and for me
to claim even a portion of it
is to be their servant.

The Last Frost Fair

was something to be happy about,
wasn't it? Four days in a short cold month

when even one's breath, upon exit,
instantly condensed into a shower of snow.

The sky was black. The river shone,
a marble corridor dulled by its awestruck traffic—

charred coal, crushed underfoot and smeared
the length of this vast, dim spine of ice

dubbed City Street by the amused vendors
—as if those walking there, terrified to drop

too bold a footfall, slid booth to booth
instead. Banked fires hurled sooty issue

against the frigid air so that smoke hung
nearly gelatinous, in wreaths of drab warmth

from Blackfriars Bridge to Three Cranes Stairs;
it was difficult to breathe. Games abounded—

skittles for the squeamish, bowling for the bold,
donkey rides for the ladies and dancing for all.

A small sheep was roasted whole on the ice
and plates and knives laid out, with penny loaves;

also an elephant led across the river by rope
just below Blackfriars—wasn't that

a sign? The Fair began on a Tuesday,
followed by Candlemas, which meant

even if the coaches still weren't running
the northern roads and yet another man

was found frozen near Dove's Inn, having
drunk freely there, then fallen into a snowbank—

all the same, winter's grip was loosening. Soon
there'd be no more sleighs-for-hire come evening,

no more Punch and no Judy duking it out
for the children crowding the makeshift stalls;

and as for the three men propped up
on hay bales when the gin tent broke loose

and skimmed downriver—
before ice water sluiced over their boots

and the sweat broke out, wasn't it
the best damn drunk ever?

From Temple to Westminster, a curve of soft fire
alive on the ice. Lanterns bobbing. No time

for din and rabble when the King was calling,
when one was nearly a Professor of Music, when . . .

Christ, the night's bitter.
Move on, before you start to enjoy

freezing to death.

V

NOMADIA

Oh that I had wings like a dove! for then would I fly away and be at rest.

—Psalms 55:6

Half-Life

Dull
the days before me,
slack the reins, my horse run off.
What a fable—
to be dunked in kisses,
sprinkled with doubts,
then slathered with high-holy
redundance.

I'm a shadow in sunlight,
unable to blush
or whiten in winter.
Beautiful monster,
where to next—
when you can hear
the wind howl
behind you, the gate

creaking shut?

Life in London, Now Playing at the Adelphi

Starring Billy Waters as Himself

Let them swagger. He can see what
they're up to, with their loopy gestures
and loud poetry, calculated and mean.
Better to be laughed at inside the theater
than out on the pitch—here's warmth,
finally, and raucous applause spilling down
from the rows of cramped arabesques
thicker than a general's chest. Let Dusty Bob
boo hoo over the pratfalls of African Sal
while yours truly fiddles, keeping time with
his good wood leg—laughter, when it comes,
is a slap in the face only if he deigns
to turn them that particular cheek.

Still, a buck's always a buck.
He'll wait in the wings, with his half-talent
and disguised ambition; he'll take on
the chores they toss at him with nary a squeak—
pull curtains, fill buckets of sand, mop up
vomit in the boxes at the interval
then lurch backstage in time to fasten
Jerry's waistcoat, straighten Tom's buffoon ruff.
He'll become indispensable, so that someday
he can dispense with those who've kept him
close by, out of habit; he'll fiddle and stomp and haul slop
until they think him inconsequential,
and he will hate them all the more for believing it.

So that's the world's jig: Fall in step
or be left behind; hop to it—*Please, sir,*
the aisles are for circulating; relieve yourself
elsewhere. As if there's an elsewhere
to get to around here.

Moor with Emeralds

Great love needs a servant,
but you don't know how to use your servants.
                    —*Leonard Cohen*, Beautiful Losers

Dear Master, Dear Dear Master,

    Do not sigh so heavily, do not droop
    into Mad Melancholy, look up!
    I am here to serve. I await
    a Word—any word!—that I may
    set down before you an array of Nature's
    most flagrant Outbursts, heaped Evidence
    of Fortunes fought for and won.

    Who can sit nursing Gloom when bathed
    in the green Fires of Phantasmagoria?
    Think of it! Smile upon
    my jagged Darlings, these ruptured Sweets
    I lift up, fresh for your gazing!

    You may think me a mere charcoal coolie,
    yet I bear such beautiful Redundance!
    I am its jubilant Negro,
    its incandescent Indian;
    I am muscled in pearwood,
    draped in garnets and almandine,
    I glisten with Fortitude!
    I stand rinsed—yes!—with Joy,
    a Holy Messenger buoyed
    by a chorus of Hallelujahs,
    all in praise of this Platter of Emeralds.

And so We are Yours now, Sire.
I will say it a thousand times
if I must—I can!—for I have
been waiting all my Life to step into
this Moment, *your* Moment,
arms full—

    Yr. most
    humble
    obedient
    exuberant
    Servant,
        O.

Vanities

As if music were a country,
he'd filled the biggest assembly rooms
on the busiest square of the capital city;
he'd played the best parties,
saw Beau Brummel blast protocol
with a single non-nod of his chin.
That had been during *his* concert season,
when everyone was buzzing;
he had owned the Pall Mall,
didn't that count for something?

Music: Coach wheels slithering,
giggles jouncing the cream cups
brimming from milady's bustier;
fear masked as delight. Music:
his Papa, his lost mother tongue.
Music: winds howling down
the four corridors of Fate
as he scrabbles after paper scraps,
tumbles the length of wherever he turned
getting longer, clutching air, crying out
(but soundlessly, a non-shout):

I played that once.
I played that once.
I played that once.

Haydn's Head

I

Haydn's head has gone missing!
When Prince Antón the Magnificent
ordered the remains exhumed
from the Hundsthurm village graveyard
to the Mountain Church crypt at Eisenstadt,

one of the footmen stumbled;
the oaken lid shivered loose—
and only the wig fell out.

II

Caution? Goes without saying.
Caution was the least of it; one needs
luck and timing, heft and a whetted blade
plus a moon obscured by clouds or calendar
to make the witching hour ring true.
We'd done it once—shoveled fearfully,
past all endurance, only to find
removal of the head from its trunk
the most taxing. This time Jungmann brought
rope in a sack and Peter a bottle of wine
and I, Joseph Carl Rosenbaum,
former employee of the Esterházy princes,
now independent businessman,
music lover and amateur phrenologist,
paid off the gravedigger. All went smoothly,

yet I felt as though I had failed
once it tumbled—so light!—into my palms.

I was prepared for the smell.
Vomited, got on with it. Stowed the prize
in a pail, hidden under lap rugs
I had tucked in the carriage;
and for that one endless journey
cradled the reek, the dread stink
of my abomination.

III

Three days in lye had reduced the smell
but still we did not dare to open the shutters
even though it was *the dead of night.*
(Joking helped ease the nausea.)
Peter looked the very part of an avenging angel
in his white hospital gown, bone saw
held aloft to deliver last rites.
Unlike the actress whose wretched leavings
we'd practiced on last autumn (ten days gone,
a medical eternity), all here was intact
and uniformly green—like a huge rose-cabbage,
heroic on its stem.

IV

Do not ask *why*,
for they would answer
"Science"—as if Science
were solely the desire
to know.

V

Materials used:
- one copper kettle
- three enamel pans
- sal ammoniac and lye (for debridement)
- spirit lamp
- spatula, trowels
- flat-nose pliers
- bone saw and a set of files
- calipers, gouges
- a good stomach
& a clear head.

VI

We ordered a box with handles—
lacquered black, fringed,
with golden lyres on either end

and lined in white taffeta—
as snug a pillow for last dreams
as any Pharaoh's. Maestro,

you would have understood.
You would not have faulted us
for using what you no longer needed.

VII

The Prince merely wished
his faithful Conductor returned
to be kept safe in death
as he was in life.
What's wrong with that?

VIII

Preliminary examinations confirmed
the prediction of an expansive cranial cavity,
every bit as persuasive in its stripped state
as when arrayed in the jellied tissues of the living.

Vivisection lasted approximately one hour,
with no difficulties except in extraction
through the nasal passages. Finally,
success: a capacious, trilling cage.

Of the twenty-seven faculties
and their corresponding positions
on Gall's phrenological map,
the protuberance for Kindness

was easily pinpointed. Also prodigious,
as expected, was the bump for Music.
Perseverance, Valour, and Circumspection
all boasted meaningful prominences

consistent with his humble assuredness,
the calm yet piercing quality of his gaze.

IX

Come on: Ten years I've kept
proof of genius safe in a lacquer box,
and now I'm to give up my dearest trophy
on the strength of one sanctimonious aristocrat's
whim for ceremony? Let him send his goons around.
I may be Suspect Number One, but there are latitudes
no man dare breach: When they come
I'll have a sick wife lying abed behind doors
—fevered princess atop her precious pea!—
while I confess in exchange for ablution.
In their eyes, one skull's as good as the next:
They'll get an anonymous old bean,
just ripe for deification.

X

The great stone was unscrewed and a brass plate
inscribed with the venerable name
taken by the Provost of the *Bergkirche*
into the inner chamber. Two days later,
the crypt aired out, he returned
utterly alone to set the head
into its rightful berth.
The sexton helped screw the stone back in place.
Every church in Eisenstadt tolled its bells.

Birthday Stroll on the Pall Mall

"February 29," 1822

A gold-capped cane reached out
and tripped me.
I did not holler.
Children pointed, cackling like crows.
I did not whimper.

Birds whose names I never knew
in Polish, German, English—not even
the *lingua franca* of my beloved opera—
twirled merrily
in the tops of the plane trees.

My heart seized up but I did not flinch.

Except a man, once . . .
I must stop thinking
this . . . a man I loved,
who like a father loved me
in the only tongue
I could claim to understand,
split me like a capon,
ripped my life—my legacy!—in two
for the sake of what he refused
to call
       A Cunt.

The birds persist with their untimely twitter.
He is deaf now, he hears nothing
of this fractured existence.
I would tell him (if he would see me)
there is no hero
who does not fall from grace;
I would whisper in his useless ear

This is the way of the world:
after the shout, a murmur;
after the murmur, a groan;
after the groan . . . ach,
worse than death
those
broken sounds.

Staffordshire Figurine, 1825

I say, old chap, where have you been?
—"Black Billy's been a-buskering
on his one good leg; the other
stayed behind in hock, marking time:
And-a-one, and-a-two, and-a-hup-hup-four,
So sorry to have lost the war!"

He's not here, son of a no-name minx, the air
is silenced. Puttied in place, secure, well lit,
the gate-mouthed raconteur holds court
whose birth and death were nothing more
than quick noise on a fiddle. Busker. Player
who'll never get to see this lacquered likeness,
street ghost who gave no care beyond
the raining down of dull brown coin.

An urban tale, nothing new.
One more sour drop in the Thames
won't stop the river's muddy traffic;
a cursed life remains doomed even when
the fortunate find they miss those antics
which forced a blush or grin.
                            How else explain
this collector's fantasy, a pantheon
gathered from niche and mantelpiece,
motley assembly of homespun Penates
unique to the common English household?
How else translate Billy's military drag
into a gaudy clump of earthenware?

What's left to say? He served
at sea, acquired a leg there, returned
and learned to scrape his catgut clean.
Got married, spawned two souls, clambered
up into the footlights for his fifteen
minutes, then fell into drink and debt;

was elected "King of the Beggars"
during his last ten days,
spent at St. Giles' Workhouse.

He was forty-five. The rest
is shrouded in that profoundest
of neglects, the haze
of centuries.

Nomadia

1825–1827, 1828–?, 1840–1848

Leavetaking

In search of pasture, a place to lie down in.
Back to the mother breast
or a dream of return
to the land of the fathers, a land my father
never mentioned, although he could pearl it out
in his impeccable German: *Vaterland.*

Fatherland, mothertongue.
I live, speak
elsewhere. This island.

St. Cloud, Paris

Strange name for a man of God. Stranger
this clipped, glazed landscape
which emerged from his modest
retreat: a man
who wished only to be
left alone—and was made
a saint for it, and brought back
into the fold. He kept vigil

here. Strange yet woefully apt then
this falling dream of water,
silver plunge and misted bursts,
swoon over swoon
tumbling

ecstatic, endless . . .
                                    as slippery as
the apparition of multiplying selves
caught in the mirror-lined rooms where
I obliged the King's morning *toilette*:
Clementi and Bach spilling
like perfume over the tossed silks,
valets tugging, murmuring over
his grunts as I kept fiddling,
tumbling smaller
and further
away . . .
                        if a saint couldn't do it,
how could I?

Strangest of all, to imagine
the tattoo of boots crossing the parquet,
bayonet-flash clattering in the constant gleam
of the gilt tabouret, the stands of agate and polished marquetry.
That among these glittering *bijoux*
Republics were proclaimed,
and emperors . . .
where now a park lies
open to the ordinary citizen:
green terraces
for the parched wayfarer.

en route

       Air, breathe me in. Take this thick
       heartache, this wily, gelatinous yearning
       and make me everywhere
       a nothingness.
                  I will be

       without boundaries, then;
       an infestation of humors, invisible companion:
       ageless, like a child.

       No one will be able to avoid me.

Rome

       I don't know the name of the tree
       which dandles here, nor of these blossoms'
       impossible exuberance, how delicate how bold.

       I should know these things.
       I should walk more, sit in the sun.

       Everyone here seems drunk from kissing.
       Noon's high light.

en route

What's left for this palm to cradle,
these fingers to promenade?
My chin, what's there for it to nudge into song;
and my chest—what about its shadow?

Dresden

Same drizzling encrustations of stone, same watery light
until darkness rolls in from the East like an army.
Sausages dangling from carts, nested in fists;
pale, stout faces fortified by the pledge to melt
once the lamps ignite in the beer halls . . .

Come to think of it, not a bad way
to dissolve the day.

The Channel

Back, back. But not
the beginning, not where
I started. That died with
Johann setting out
on the road. That died
when the only language I trusted
began to grow under my fingers
from the humming wood.

London

What am I looking for?
Why? I look and look, at people,
horses, even plants in the royal gardens at Kew—
I am tired of my eyes, I am tired of my ears,
my fingers itch for music but I am tired of
hearing it. Why not taste
then, or touch—that's a good sense,
the Lilliputian topography of a lace handkerchief,
the cool slide of a marble hip . . .
There I go, buzzing around the edges of things,
never a person, never a heart I can feel
swelling in this lover's chest, never skin. . . .
Once I felt I could walk a straight line
out of this city into the next
free world. But smell attacks
like a phalanx of grenadiers, so swiftly
from there to here to inside
and before you know it,
the citadel is lost.

Strolling

Real World, the one where everyone
exclaims how fortunate I am to have lived
amid such benign, beautiful people—weren't they
wise and generous and kind, aren't I grateful?
They were, they were, they were

and I am.

Along the Serpentine, Hyde Park

Violettengeruch:
a made-up word,
melancholy, blunt—
unlike its glib English cousin
scent-of-violets,
or the easy solace of refining
odeur to *parfum*;
yet none of these
—flippant, vulgar, smooth—
equal to the terror
a clutch of violets engenders
stumbled upon at dusk,
that panics the senses: so
sweet, so cold.

Self-Eulogy

Finally the verdict's
Come through.
All the pots licked
For their stew
Lie empty, cold;
Soon the last copper coin will arrive. . . .
But, dear Papa—I've
Tasted the gold.

#8 Victory Cottages, Peckham, 1860

"Tot ist tot."

Not true, what the living claim we regret in the last hour:
no memories worth blubbering through, nor scrabbling for favor
in the eyes of our children, nor honor sought among friends.
Drool travels unnoticed from collar to pillow while, suspended
by blankets, a thigh dangles, blameless and bare.
Shame has lost its sting in this penultimate hell,
these next-to-last days when we're still "ourselves."

I don't need wine or gossip or weather, I don't give a fig
for warm socks or—don't laugh—the summer's first pear,
a fruit I haven't been able to digest for twenty years
and have mourned for as long. What's any of it
compared to this draining of humors, this wondrous uncaring?
Pain's an interference; Love is cumbersome. For I loved only
what my fingers could do, and even they did not serve me
forever.

The Witness

Yeah, that's him, Bridgetower.
Didn't know his given name.
George, eh? Like the King.
Fancy, fancy for that sour
pint of breath he was wheezing.

Half-blood and all, though,
I didn't mind him. Dusty, a bit;
I couldn't help brushing my sleeve
after greeting—afraid he'd sprinkle
some of that brown my way.

Sorry. It ain't right
to make fun of the fresh dead—
newly—naw, I mean to say
late, departed—you know,
them that's just cooling. . . .

So he was a fiddler,
something of a stunner in his day.
"Day's done, gone the sun"—
ain't that a German song? Heard it
somewhere. Kinda mournful.

Wonder could he play that.

EPILOGUES

Who tracks the steps of glory to the grave?
—Lord Byron

If you want a happy ending, that depends, of course, on where you stop your story.
—Orson Welles

The Queen's Wardrobe Keeper

Mrs. Papendiek's Diary (5)

Dimity, elderberry, shawl and muff,
husband, children, grandchildren—
undinting service, no questions asked.
Remember the time the coach let you out
at the wrong station and you fell
crossing the meadow—how
the mud stain on your puce silk riled you less
than the put-out glare in the eyes of your host?

Ah, Charlotte. Did any stranger
other than the Queen you served
ever call you by name? Would you
have so desired it? Some say your diaries—
recollected forty years after the fact
at the urging of your children,
who thought it a proper "amusement"
for passing time during an illness—
provide anecdotal insights into life
at the Hanoverian court. Anecdotal,
as in having no bearing on world events.
Inconsequential theater, minutia,
silly stuff all in a day's work—but
your day, your life.

All That Jazz

The African Prince

I fashioned a person to inhabit.
He was high maintenance
but so was I; we set each other ticking.
It was beautiful to watch as long
as you stayed out of the way.

I dropped in on the wife,
whored around the Continent for a while,
caught a cold hiding on a lady's balcony
and went straight to the mineral baths of Karlovy Vary,
where I taught English to schoolboys
and wooed their mother in French. I hitched
a carriage-ride to the banks of the Kneiper,
where it was rumored Catherine the Great
was trolling for eels . . . *ach*, who cares

where I've been, where I came from,
where I went? All that matters in life
is joy—and joy (like me) is a traveling man.
I died on the way to Prague.

The Composer's Coda

Ludwig van B.

I wanted fame. I wanted love.
I deserved bliss but bliss
scares easily.

I fled Bonn's dreary terrain
for Vienna's grave lilt:
There I learned to cherish
even the gaps, the static.

Fame became moot.
Love, a strategy.

Beauty was what I couldn't seem
to hang on to. Beauty would
discharge her blandishments,
then retreat to observe the effect.

Now I know none of this is real,
none of this exists.
That next moment,
shimmering before you? Wink—

and it will either astonish you
or be gone.

Haydn's Skull

And so it occurred in the year 1809
that gravedigger Jakob Demuth, paid handsomely,
handed over the prize to perpetrators
Michael Jungmann, Johann Nepomuk Peter,
and Joseph Carl Rosenbaum; that Rosenbaum,
former footman to the Prince and amateur phrenologist,
squirreled this, his most treasured possession, away
for years, even in face of the discovery,
the abduction and subsequent investigation
by the Prince's guards, stuffing the mattress
just in time to declare his innocence
while his wife tossed in feigned fever on a lumpy bed;
and that the rogue Rosenbaum remained in possession
until his death; whereupon,
acting in accord to his testament

his widow (the erstwhile princess on the pea)
passed on this strange glory to Johann Nepomuk Peter,
who on his deathbed bequeathed it to
his clueless physician, Karl Haller,
who trusted Doctor Carl von Rokitansky,
curator of the Imperial Pathological Museum,
to know what to do. He did. He kept it.
Held on until 1895, when he himself
was dispatched to dust and the composer's skull given
to the Viennese Society of Music Lovers,
devoted to keeping the music which had issued

from that head alive, and in whose museum
it reposed for sixty more years
before the reunion of body and soul found consecration
in Prince Esterházy's Haydn Mausoleum
at the *Bergkirche* in Eisenstadt, in 1954.

historical

The Name Game

George Augustus Polgreen Bridgetower

Will the real name please stand up?
Not the geographical marker (*look for
a bridge, a tower; that is the place*)
or the stamp of shame that is Bridgetown,
complete with slave compounds and a dramatic escape.
George! To please the King, every second son
was stuck with George somewhere in their monikers,
while Augustus lent a hint of classical bragging rights.

What's in a name is what you put in it;
the concealment's all in a day's work.
Here, only the middle name, odd
as it is, seems real. Clumsy Polgreen,
sticking out, refusing to move.
Poland Forever? A large conifer?
A staff to lean on, the flowering rod of Moses?

We'll never know. Just as we'll never know
if the day that doesn't exist
was the day he was born,
or the day he died,
or both.

Instrumental

A stick.
A string.
A bow.

The twang
as the arrow
leaves it.

The twang
praising
the imprint

it makes
on the air,
caressing

the breach
no one sees
shivering

struck

The End, with MapQuest

Will I cry for you, Polgreen? Will I drag out your end
though it is long past, though I drove slowly past
the place of your dying days and recorded
what I knew I'd find there—
families in townhouses, a sensible Vauxhall
parked askew in the carport behind the green grate?
Will I tell you, whispering to no one in particular
how even the street sign seemed greasy,
and that it was raining, natch, and whenever
I tried to focus on the thought of you
laid out in one of those miserable Victory cottages
(no turrets! no gilded palms! no jiggling regents!)
I had to do something, crack a joke or snap
another useless photo of the Bellenden Primary School,
but when we turned left to round the block
for the fifth time, it was the perfectly dismal
sight of a fast-food joint on the corner,
Sam's Kebabs, which cheered me. Would you understand?
The red and yellow neon script, shouting
like a Janissary band, so tacky it was buoyant,
colorful because there was no good reason
to be afraid of shouting with the whole world
determined not to hear you,
though they tried to shut you up all the time.

Do I care enough, George Augustus Bridgetower,
to miss you? I don't even know if I really like you.
I don't know if your playing was truly gorgeous
or if it was just you, the sheer miracle of all
that darkness swaying close enough to *touch*,
palm tree and Sambo and glistening tiger
running circles into golden oil. Ah,
Master B, little great man, tell me:
How does a shadow shine?

Notes

"PARIS, PANTING" / "WHAT DOESN'T HAPPEN" George Augustus Polgreen Bridgetower's debut—playing a concerto by Giovanni Giornovichi—was one of the last concerts given by a foreigner in the Concert spirituel series before the French Revolution broke out and changed Parisian life forever. The Concert spirituel (1725–1790), one of the very first public concert series, had switched venues from the enormous Salle des Cent Suisses (Hall of the Hundred Swiss Guards) to the equally cavernous stage of the Salle des Machines, both situated in the Tuileries Palace. Built by the great Catherine de Medici and used as a temporary residency by Louis XIV during the construction of Versailles, the Tuileries Palace served mainly as a theater until the Revolution, when the royal family was placed under house arrest there. Napoleon I made it his primary residence, restoring it to official status until its destruction by the Supports of the Commune in 1871.

Before leaving the Continent for England, Bridgetower played at several other venues in Paris—notably the May 27, 1789, concert at the Panthéon, with Thomas Jefferson in attendance.

"MRS. PAPENDIEK'S DIARY (1–4)" Mrs. Papendiek, Assistant Keeper of the Wardrobe and Reader to Her Majesty Queen Charlotte, was persuaded by her grandchildren to write down her account of the long last years in the reign of King George III. Her husband was not only head page at court but an accomplished amateur musician (violin, flute) as well, and took an active interest in Polgreen.

"THE MARINE PAVILION, BRIGHTHELMSTON" The Prince of Wales poured a fortune—and most of his adult life—into the creation of his own version of Graceland in the seaside resort of Brighton, where he would spend summers carousing with his uncle, the Duke of Cumberland (King George III's younger brother). Renovations on the farmhouse fated to become that "masterpiece of bad taste" known as "the Folly at Brighton" began in 1787; the next three and a half decades would see wings added, porticoes plotted, water closets and heating systems installed, stables erected, and rooms re-outfitted to reflect the Prince's shifting infatuations with French neoclassicism, chinoiserie, and Mogul India.

"THE SEASIDE CONCERTS"   Rauzzini's critique is taken from the December 8, 1789, edition of the *Bath Morning Post*. Rauzzini doesn't leave it at that, however; he complicates the effusion by insulting an old friend, the violinist La Motte, in the process, asserting that La Motte was "much inferior to this wonderful boy." Ouch! That's gotta hurt.

"JANISSARY RAP"   Dressed in the lavish garb of an imaginary Levant— balloon trousers, sashes, and plumed turbans—these African musicians marched through London, flashing tambourines and jingling "Johnny-bells," a type of glockenspiel festooned with ribbons.

"ABANDONED, AGAIN"   The African Prince has gone gaming again. His son flees to Carlton House, London residence of the Prince of Wales—who's hardly an improvement upon the elder Bridgetower; but at least there'll be more room to get lost in.

"THE TRANSACTION"   Carlton House, 1791. Upon hearing of *Pere* Bridgetower's dissolute habits, the Prince of Wales—no Eagle Scout himself—pays the father to leave England and so becomes the boy's legal guardian. The price? £25—which, lest we become indignant, translates to $4,157.44 in today's currency. Still.

"BROTHERS IN SPRING"   George's younger brother Ferdinand was a cellist; his name appears on several London concert programs during this time.

"THE SALOMON CONCERTS"   George will eventually serve fourteen years as first violinist in the Prince of Wales's orchestra, performing at the Prince's home in London and at the Royal Pavilion in Brighton.

"NEW CENTURY AUBADE"   According to the Gregorian calendar, leap years are divisible by four and add an extra day (February 29). A solar year, however, is slightly shorter than this calendar calculation (365.25 days); in order to keep in sync with the solar system, yet another adjustment must be made, to wit: Years evenly divisible by 100 are not leap years unless they are also divisible by 400. This would make 1600 and 2000 leap years, while 1700, 1800, and 1900 were not. Ergo: No birthday in 1800 for George Bridgetower; he must wait until 1804 for another February 29.

"THE PETITION"   George applies for a leave of absence from the Prince's orchestra in order to visit his ailing mother in Saxony.

"OLD WORLD LULLABY"   All this time, George's mother Maria Anna has been living in the city of Dresden, on an annual pension from the Prince of Wales.

"FLOATING REQUIEM"   Records show George and his brother performing together in Dresden between July 1802 and March 1803.

"LUDWIG VAN BEETHOVEN'S RETURN TO VIENNA"   On doctor's orders, Beethoven spends the summer of 1802 in the village of Heiligenstadt. That autumn, as he prepares to return for Vienna's musical season, he writes a letter to his brothers Carl and Johann (known as the Heiligenstadt Testament) in which he despairs over his hearing loss, confesses his aspirations and fears, and puts his affairs in order.

"FIRST CONTACT"   On April 16, 1803, Beethoven runs into Count Prichowsky on the street and spontaneously invites him and his walking companion (Johann Held, a physician from Prague and amateur musician) to Schuppanzigh's rooms, where some of the composer's piano works that had been transcribed for string quartet were to be rehearsed. According to Dr. Held, among the musicians present (and presumably taking part) were Wenzel Krumpholtz, Johann Nepomuk Möser, and "the mulatto Bridgethauer."

"BEETHOVEN SUMMONS HIS COPYIST"   Ferdinand Ries (1784–1838) came from Bonn to Vienna in order to study pianoforte with Beethoven. He rapidly became an unofficial amanuensis, copying out scores whenever the regular copyist was not available (which, thanks to the composer's last-minute inspirations, was often the case), alternately serving as an impromptu walking companion, surrogate son, and eventually, inadvertent biographer.

"AUGARTEN, 7 AM"   The Augarten concerts were held every Sunday throughout the summer months—an opportunity to catch a whiff of green, to see and be seen: "Now the season of music had arrived." (Julius Wilhelm Fischer)

"GEORGIE PORGIE, OR A MOOR IN VIENNA"   The Austrians are notorious for their delicately warped humor—occasionally obscene, sometimes coarse, always outrageous. No icon, beloved or feared or revered, was exempt; social satire flourished in an unremitting stream of farces one could file under the rubric Travesties of Great Literature. (Think Punch and Judy, with human punching bags and much better puns.) In the first half of the nineteenth century alone, Vienna theaters mounted multiple parodic versions of works by Shakespeare, Goethe, Schiller, Rossini, and Mozart—just to name a few of the more international figures—with *Hamlet, Othello,* and *The Sorrows of Young Werther* taking top honors.

The Prater, Vienna's famed recreational area, had already become a favorite escape from dust and city traffic; but the park's most famous landmark was still to come: Hubert Cecil Booth erected his *Riesenrad* (giant wheel) in 1897.

"RAIN"   Vienna: June 1803. Beethoven has retracted his dedication to Bridgetower. By this time he really can't hear much of anything. What is the sound of one raindrop falling?

"TAIL TUCKED"   His prospects in ruin, our upstart hero turns tail on Vienna. Beethoven, noted for his intransigence, would not recall his repudiation of the brilliant violinist who had saved the composer's hide by improvising the cadenzas in the new sonata. Bitter? You betcha. And all because young George had put the moves on some Skirt. As if Big B. would've had a snowball's chance in the matter.

"THE COUNTESS SHARES CONFIDENCES . . ."   The legendary beauty Countess Giulietta Guicciardi arrived in Vienna in 1800. Of course Beethoven fell in love with her, even though the difference in their social status ruled out all hope. Three years later she married Wenzel Robert Gallenberg, a mediocre composer but a bona fide Count. After a swift assessment of the marriage, the freshly anointed Countess von Wallenberg remained true to class by managing a love affair with a prince. At least we got the "Moonlight Sonata" out of the bargain.

"CAMBRIDGE, GREAT ST. MARY'S CHURCH" As the crowning achievement in fulfillment of the Bachelor's degree in music, GPB's own composition is performed at Great St. Mary's Church.

"PANOPTICON" The Panopticon, designed by Jeremy Bentham in 1791, became the blueprint for penal systems, providing a unique and unsettling solution for optimal monitoring of inmates. Cell blocks were arrayed in stacked octagons, with each building forming a phalanx that radiated from a central tower, like a giant pinwheel; guard lookouts were situated at the hub of each octagon, with the warden's office posted at the very core of this macabre flower. Construction on Millbank Prison (on the left bank of the Thames, near Vauxhall Bridge) began in 1812.

"MOOR WITH EMERALDS" The sculpture known as Moor with Emerald Cluster is part of the treasury display in the famous Green Vaults of Dresden's Residence Palace, the Zwinger. A collaboration between Baroque/Rococo sculptor Balthasar Permoser (1651–1732) and court jeweler Johann Melchior Dinglinger (1664–1731), the wooden figure is twenty-five inches tall, encrusted with silver, gold, rubies, sapphires, topazes, garnets, and carries on a tortoiseshell tray the largest emerald cluster in the world. True to his vocation's credo of excess, goldsmith Dinglinger married five times and had twenty-three children.

"BIRTHDAY STROLL ON THE PALL MALL" After an unseasonably mild winter, the birds have returned early. Is it February or March? 1822 is not a leap year, so technically it's March 1—which means poor George has no real birthday to celebrate.

"STAFFORDSHIRE FIGURINE, 1825" The founding father of the Brighton Museum, Mr. Henry Willett (1823–1903), may have earned his fortune through astute management of the family brewery, but his true passion—collecting—would earn him a place in posterity. He believed that "the history of a country may be traced on its homely pottery"; his Collection of Popular Pottery features over two thousand ceramic pieces covering aspects of British nineteenth-century life, including figurines of George III and George IV, Queen Caroline, Lord Byron, Mr. Pickwick, African Sal, and Black Billy Waters.

A Chronology

1780   29 *Feb*   George Augustus Polgreen Bridgetower* is born in Biala (Poland/Saxony) to Friedrich Augustus Bridgetower (Caribbean/African) and Maria Anna (Polish/German)

1780–   Friedrich Bridgetower serves as personal page to Prince
1789   Esterházy (aka "Miklós the Magnificent")

         Franz Josef Haydn is musical director of the Esterházy estate at Esterháza (now in Hungary)

1784   Ferdinand Ries, composer, is born

         Thomas Jefferson arrives in Paris, followed by his daughter Martha and her personal slave, Sally Hemings

1785   10 *Mar*   Thomas Jefferson becomes U.S. Minister (ambassador) to France

      15 *Dec*   The Prince of Wales marries Mrs. Fitzherbert in an "illegal" ceremony in her London drawing rooms

1789   11 *Apr*   GPB's professional debut, at the prestigious Concert spirituel in Paris

* hereafter designated as GPB

	14 July	Storming of the Bastille
	Sept	Thomas Jefferson leaves Paris for the United States
	pre-Oct	GPB performs at Windsor
	13 Oct	GPB's London debut, a private concert at the Papendieks
	5–8 Dec	GPB gives concerts in Bath & Bristol
1790	*2 Jan*	Mozart's opera *Così Fan Tutte* premieres in Vienna
	19 Feb	GPB's first public concert in London, Drury Lane Theatre
		> A mild winter <
	2 June	GPB and Franz Clement (1780–1843), violin prodigy from Austria, perform at the Hanover Square Rooms, London
	28 Sept	Miklós I dies. His successor, Antón Esterházy, disbands orchestra and choir, keeping only the military band—whereupon Haydn quits after twenty-nine years of service and leaves for Vienna
	Dec	Johann Peter Salomon, violinist and concert promoter, comes to Vienna to lure Haydn to London
	15 Dec	Haydn and Salomon set out on seventeen-day journey to London; French Revolution continues to rage
1791	*1 Jan*	Haydn and Salomon arrive in England: The white cliffs of Dover!
		Friedrich Bridgetower is ordered to leave England; the Prince of Wales becomes GPB's official guardian
	Mar–June	The Salomon concert series introduces new work by

Haydn to the London musical scene

	30 Sept	Mozart's *Magic Flute* premieres in Vienna
	5 Dec	Mozart dies in Vienna
1792	*summer*	Haydn leaves London, returns to Vienna
1793	*21 Jan*	Louis XVI of France is executed
	1 Feb	Great Britain declares war on France
	10 Aug	The Louvre, originally a fortress in the Tuilleries complex, officially opens its doors as the Museum Central des Arts
	26 Oct	Marie Antoinette is executed
1794	*Jan*	Haydn returns to London
	10 Feb	Salomon's second concert series begins with a première of Haydn's Symphony No. 99 in E-flat Major
		Upon Antón Esterházy's death, Nicolas (II) assumes princely title and asks Haydn to return
		GPB benefit concert for Spitalfields weavers
	23 June	Prince of Wales separates from Mrs. Fitzherbert
	6 Nov	GPB concert in Salisbury (playing a concerto in the style of Viotti)
1795	*8 Apr*	The Prince of Wales marries his German cousin Caroline
	15 Aug	Haydn leaves London for the last time

>A dry year; especially hot & dry September<

	26 Oct	Napoleon Bonaparte becomes Commander of the French Army
1796	7 Jan	Princess Charlotte is born to the Prince of Wales and his wife; a scant five months later, Prince George separates from Caroline
1797	14 Jan	Napoleon defeats Austria in Rivoli (northern Italy)
1798		Rudolphe Kreutzer spends two months in Vienna, meets Beethoven
		Napoleon annexes Egypt
1798–1799		GPB plays Covent Garden, Drury Lane, and Haymarket theatres
1799	12 Mar	Austria declares war on France
	summer	The Prince of Wales forces Mrs. Fitzherbert to return to him
	9 Nov	Napoleon Bonaparte declares himself Dictator of France
1800		Due to astronomical time adjustments, no leap year, no birthday; GPB remains "four" years old
		Countess Giulietta Guicciardi arrives in Vienna, receives piano instruction from Beethoven
1801		Beethoven composes "Moonlight Sonata" for Countess Guicciardi
	24 Apr	Haydn's oratorio Die Jahreszeiten (The Seasons) premieres in Vienna
1802	May	Great Britain declares war on France

2 Aug	French Senate declares Napoleon Bonaparte Consul for Life
6 Oct	Beethoven writes the Heiligenstadt Testament
24 July–Mar 1803	GPB performs (with brother Ferdinand) in Dresden, Teplitz, and Carlsbad
1803	GPB arrives in Vienna sometime between Mar 18 (his last documented Dresden concert) and April
Apr	GPB meets Beethoven
24 May	GPB premieres Beethoven's Violin Sonata No. 9 in A Major, Opus 47, in the Augarten Pavilion series, with the composer on piano
July	GPB leaves Vienna, visits the Esterházy estate at Eisenstadt
end of July	GPB visits his mother in Dresden, before returning to England
3 Nov	Countess Guicciardi marries Count Wenzel Robert Gallenberg, composer of ballet and occasional music
1804	Haydn officially resigns his post to Prince Esterházy
	Beethoven finishes *Eroica* at Jezeri, Lobkowitz's Bohemian castle
18 May	French Senate proclaims Napoleon Bonaparte emperor; enraged, Beethoven tears up the dedication page of his Third Symphony (the *Eroica*)
2 Dec	Napoleon crowns himself emperor, Notre Dame Cathedral

	20 Dec	United States buys Louisiana Territory from France
1805	Apr	Beethoven's Violin Sonata No. 9 published with the dedication: "al suo amico R. Kreutzer"
	26 May	Napoleon is crowned King of Italy
1806	27 Oct	Napoleon marches into Berlin
	3 Dec	Franz Clement premieres Beethoven's Violin Concerto (which he commissioned) at Theater an der Wien
1807	28 Jan	London's Pall Mall becomes the first street lit by gaslight
1808	21 May	Eston Hemings is born to Sally Hemings at Monticello
1809	13 May	Napoleon invades Vienna and stations guards around Haydn's home; Haydn counters by playing the Austrian national anthem once a day, loudly
	31 May	Haydn dies in his sleep, shortly after midnight
1811	5 Jan	The Prince of Wales ("Prinny" to his friends) becomes prince regent after his father, George III, slips into permanent dementia
	19 June	Regency Fete at Carlton House; Mrs. Fitzherbert makes the final break with Prinny (who is partying with his new mistress, Lady Hertford)
	28 June	GPB receives Bachelor of Music degree from Cambridge
1812		Construction commences on Millbank Prison
	June	Napoleon begins his Russian Campaign

	18 Dec	Napoleon arrives in Paris with depleted troops after the Russian Campaign has turned into a disaster
1813	8 Mar	First concert of the Royal Philharmonic Society; the thirty founding members include Muzio Clementi, Johann Peter Salomon, and George Bridgetower)
	27 Aug	Napoleon is defeated in the Battle of Dresden
1814	1–4 Feb	Frost Fair in London

>among five coldest winters on record, esp. Jan–March<

	31 Mar	The Coalition army enters Paris
	11 Apr	Napoleon is banished to Elba
1815	Feb	Napoleon escapes Elba, gathers forces for new offensive
	18 June	Napoleon defeated at Waterloo
	15 July	Napoleon exiled to St. Helena
	25 Nov	Johann Peter Salomon dies
1817	18 Apr	Records show that the royal pension for GPB's mother is discontinued
		Prinny is pelted with stones in London's streets, decamps to his Marine Pavilion in Brighton more and more frequently
1820	29 Jan	George III (eighty-one years old) dies, insane, at Windsor Castle
	19 July	Coronation: The Prince of Wales becomes George IV

	7 *Nov*	Haydn's remains, minus the head, are transferred from Vienna to Eisenstadt for reinterment
1821	5 *May*	Napoleon Bonaparte dies on St. Helena, of slow arsenic poisoning
1821–23		Stage run at Adelphi Theatre of the play *Tom and Jerry, or Life in London* (by William Moncrieff); Black Billy Waters plays himself
1824	7 *May*	Premiere of Beethoven's Ninth Symphony in Vienna
1825–27		GPB in Rome
1827	26 *Mar*	Beethoven dies
1828		GPB removes himself from Royal Society of Musicians to "reside abroad"

>A WET year<

1830	26 *June*	George Augustus Frederick of Hanover, King George IV of England, aka "Prinny," dies; the locket found around his neck contains a miniature of Mrs. Fitzherbert
1833		Charlotte Papendiek begins her journal
1837		Mrs. Fitzherbert dies in Brighton
1839		Charlotte Papendiek dies

>GPB spends many years on the Continent, leaving considerably fewer traces than during his younger years<

1840		en route from Dresden to London
1845		Vienna

1846		London
1848		St. Cloud (Paris)
1860	*20 Feb*	George Augustus Polgreen Bridgetower dies in Peckham, South London, No. 8 Victory Cottages
1895		Haydn's skull is given to the Museum of the Gesellschaft der Musikfreunde, where it remains for fifty-nine years
1954		Haydn's skull is finally reinterred with his body in the crypt of the *Bergkirche* ("Mountain Church") in Eisenstadt

Acknowledgments

These poems first appeared—sometimes in slightly different versions—in the following publications:

Agni Review: "Seduction Against Exterior Pilaster, Waning Gibbous," "*Andante con Variazioni*," and "Staffordshire Figurine, 1825"

American Poetry Review: "Capriccio," "Lines Whispered to a Pillow," "Disappearance," "Brothers in Spring," "Old World Lullaby," "Home Again," and "The End, with MapQuest"

Callaloo: "Prologue of the Rambling Sort," "(Re)Naissance," "Friedrich Augustus Bridgetower Discovers the Purposes of Fatherhood," "Recollection, Preempted," "The Seaside Concerts," "The Dressing," "New Century Aubade," "To the Continent," "Ludwig van Beethoven's Return to Vienna," "First Contact," "Beethoven Summons His Copyist," "*Tafelmusik* (2)," and "The Composer's Coda"

Daedalus: "The Countess Shares Confidences over *Karneval* Chocolate"

Gettysburg Review: "Black Pearl," "Moor with Emeralds," "*Life in London*, Now Playing at the Adelphi," and "Haydn's Head"

Hunger Mountain: "Vanities," "Birthday Stroll on the Pall Mall," and "The Name Game"

The International Literary Quarterly (UK): "The Lesson: Adagio," "Instrumental," "The African Prince Sings Songs of Love," "Mrs. Papendiek's Diary

(2)," Mrs. Papendiek's Diary (4)," "Half-Life," "Cambridge, Great St. Mary's Church," "Panopticon," "#8 Victory Cottages, Peckham, 1860," and "The Witness"

The Kenyon Review: "The Wardrobe Lesson," "Janissary Rap," "Ode on a Negress Head Clock, with Eight Tunes," and "Concert at Hanover Square"

The Massachusetts Review: "Rain"

Michigan Quarterly Review: "The Marine Pavilion, Brighthelmston" and "Esterháza, Prodigal"

Mid-American Review: "Mrs. Papendiek's Diary (1)," "Mrs. Papendiek's Diary (3)," and "The Queen's Wardrobe Keeper"

The New Yorker: "The Bridgetower"

North American Review: "*Tafelmusik* (1)" and "The Last Frost Fair"

The Oxford American: "Windsor," "The Salomon Concerts," "Haydn Serenades the Napoleonic Honor Guard," and "The Regency Fete"

Parnassus: "Polgreen, Sight-Reading" and "Tail Tucked"

Shenandoah: "Pulling the Organ Stops," "Haydn, Overheard," and "Haydn's Skull"

Slate: "Haydn Leaves London" and "*Ach*, Wien"

The Southern Review: "Ode to the Moon" and "Vienna Spring"

Transition: "Hear Ye!," "The Performer," "Augarten, 7 AM," and "Eroica"

Virginia Quarterly Review: "What Doesn't Happen," "Paris, Panting," "Black Billy Waters, at His Pitch," "Pretty Boy," "Floating Requiem," and "Nomadia"

For all the encouragement and support from friends and family received during this long and sometimes arduous birthing, I am deeply grateful. Special thanks go to:

my husband, Fred Viebahn, who buoyed me when the waters were deepest, nagged when I resented it most, swore that he liked listening to violins all night, cheerfully trudged along as I attempted to match modern London via GPS with Regency-era maps, and took photographs even when I thought I didn't need them;

Diana Gunnarson, for her intrepid and shrewd research;

Peter Norton, whose summer house in Oak Bluffs afforded me the change of scenery and crucial time to outline this book;

the maintenance man at Kensal Green Cemetery who led us through the catacombs' narrow passages, stood patiently by as we stared at the marble plaque marking the position of George Augustus Polgreen Bridgetower's coffin, and whose own name I didn't catch;

my local library, supplier of innumerable plastic-jacketed mysteries for the occasional (necessary) distraction;

Edmund Najera, my voice teacher, for keeping me physically connected to the music;

and in memory of

Carol Houck Smith, my editor, who accompanied this book with her astute counsel and enthusiasm . . . but most of all, her patience—dare I say faith?—throughout its production, until her untimely death in December 2008.

Biographical Note

Rita Dove, former U.S. Poet Laureate, is the recipient of many honors, among them the Pulitzer Prize, the National Humanities Medal, the Heinz Award, and the NAACP Great American Artist Award. Among her publications are the novel *Through the Ivory Gate*, the drama *The Darker Face of the Earth*, and numerous poetry collections—most recently *American Smooth* and *On the Bus with Rosa Parks*. She is Commonwealth Professor of English at the University of Virginia.

Additional biographical information is available on the Web at www.RitaDovePoetry.com.